SURVIVAL GUIDE FOR YOUNG WOMEN

LEARNING HOW TO NAVIGATE
TODAY'S WORLD WITH
GRACE AND STRENGTH

HOLLY WAGNER | NICOLE REYES

From Gospel Light
Ventura, California, U.S.A.

For more information and
special offers from Regal Books,
email us at
subscribe@regalbooks.com

Published by Regal
From Gospel Light
Ventura, California, U.S.A.
www.regalbooks.com
Printed in the U.S.A.

Library of Congress Cataloging-in-Publication Data
Wagner, Holly.
Survival guide for young women : learning how to navigate today's world with grace and strength / Holly Wagner, Nicole Reyes.
p. cm.
Includes bibliographical references and index.
ISBN 978-0-8307-6249-1 (trade paper : alk. paper)
1. Christian women—Conduct of life. I. Reyes, Nicole. II. Title.
BJ1610.W33 2012
248.8'43—dc23
2012012411

This book is dedicated to all the young women who want to make a difference in the world. Just know that there are women who believe in you and are cheering you on!

—HOLLY

This book is dedicated to my father . . . your love and support has given me the courage to pursue with passion the purpose for my life! You mean the world to me, and I respect and love you more than words can describe! I also dedicate this book to my pastors, Philip and Holly Wagner. I would not be fulfilling the call of God on my life without your love, example and investment. Your belief in me has made all the difference in my life, and I am eternally thankful!

—NICOLE

CONTENTS

INTRODUCTION

I am sure most of us have experienced one or more "aha" moments in our lives. Let me describe one of mine.

I have read the Bible through a number of times—and I have read the book of Titus many times. However, there was a moment a few years ago when chapter 2 jumped out at me. Basically, this passage challenges older women to assume responsibility for younger women. I thought, *Great, when I get to be 103, then I will be an older woman, and I will train up all those young'uns!*

I heard a whisper from heaven: "Holly. Is there anyone younger than you on the planet?"

I had to think for a minute.

After all, I am NOT old . . . so I must be young!

But really . . . of course there is someone younger than me on the earth.

As soon as I admitted that, I heard heaven again: "Well, Holly, then you are an older woman. As long as there is someone younger than you, you are an older woman."

Wasn't sure I really wanted to be called an old woman.

In a sick way, it makes me feel better to call you an old woman, too.

And you are.

You are an old woman.

Why?

Because right now . . . in your world, there is a woman who is younger than you are.

If you are 16 . . . you are an old woman.

Why?

Because there are 10-year-olds who need to learn from you.

If you are 25 . . . you are an old woman.

Why?

Because that 16-year-old needs to know what you know.

If you are 43 . . . you are an old woman.

Why?

Because there is a 20-something who desperately needs your wisdom.

If you are 99 . . . you got all of us!

As long as there is someone younger than you on the planet, you are an older woman. And as older women, we have a responsibility. We are to equip, motivate, inspire and train younger women.

At any and every moment, you are both an older woman *and* a younger woman. You are being handed a baton and passing one off.

As the older women, we should be opening our hearts and our worlds to a younger woman . . . encouraging her, accepting her and offering her wisdom we have gained. This is not always convenient or easy . . . but it is so important!! I am to be living my life in such a way that a younger woman actually wants to follow me.

When in younger woman mode . . . we are in the position of receiving. Most of the time, this means we need to "shutteth uppeth!" We are looking for the wisdom . . . the insight . . . the help. So we probably need to be quiet and listen. I have sometimes been guilty, when in younger woman mode, of doing all the talking.

Not smart.

Sometimes we try to make excuses, defend our position, or explain away our lack of knowledge.

Bad idea.

We need to humble ourselves so that we can learn.

I have had the privilege of leading quite a few young women in the past few years. (In other words . . . I have been their older woman!) My life is richer because they are in it. One of the young women in my world is Nicole Reyes. I have worked with her for almost 10 years. I have watched her grow, make decisions, learn to "shutteth uppeth," deal with issues in her heart, and be committed to fulfilling God's purpose for her life. I have also watched her extend her heart and life to her younger women . . . being committed to seeing them fulfill God's plan. I have asked her to write this book with me, in the hopes that together our voices would bring even more wisdom.

My desire in writing this book is to share some of the things I have learned over the years. As I was writing, I asked myself, *What do I wish I had known when I was in my twenties and thirties?* That is what you will find on these pages. Some of it is fun, random nonsense. But some of it really can help you on your journey.

I am asking you to open your heart and be willing to learn. Maybe reading about my mistakes can keep you from making the same ones.

XOXO . . . HOLLY

• • • • • • •

It was less than a year ago that Holly and I sat down for lunch at one of our favorite restaurants to chat about ministry, family, guys, and the random other topics one can expect to be discussed by a couple of God Chicks doing life together! This routine had developed organically over the years, and as a younger woman gleaning from the valuable wisdom of such an inspiring older woman, I always looked forward to our time together. At this particular meeting, over a couple of salads and a couple of lattes, we began to dream about writing a book that tackled the real issues young women are facing . . . and to have fun doing it!

A rush of excitement, mixed with a profound sense of responsibility, came over me as we brought up topics like dating and career and health and discovering purpose and overcoming issues of the heart. Then we both laughed after throwing in the equally important issue of finding the perfect pair of jeans to flatter a girl's figure! ☻ We decided no topic would be off limits. We wanted to do whatever it took to truly inspire and equip young women to navigate well the seasons of life that lie ahead.

Early on in the writing process, I had my own "aha" moment. I realized that this book is more a memoir than anything else. The wisdom and experience I contribute to these pages represent what I have learned over the past 10 years, largely because of the remarkable older women and men in my world.

Holly Wagner, perhaps more than anyone, has beautifully played the role of "older woman" in my life. As my pastor, leader and friend, she has encouraged and challenged me to fulfill my God-given purpose and destiny, to never settle for less, and to laugh more along the way!

When I met Holly, I was just 19 years old . . . full of dreams and potential, along with my fair share of hurts, brokenness and just plain old stupidity. Fast forward to today . . . I am a 29-year-old single and fulfilled pastor, teacher and executive team member who oversees different teams and areas of church life. I've been able to overcome the hurts of my past and passionately pursue Jesus and His plan for my life. I'm far from perfect, but I'm committed to living out this God-adventure to the fullest, with eternity in mind!

The things I've learned as the younger woman in the years between 19 and 29 have made all the difference! I learned to forgive and overcome hurts from my childhood. I learned to communicate honor and respect to men. I learned to lead different types of people. I learned that life isn't all about me . . . and that's a good thing! I learned how to date smart. I learned how to eat healthy. I learned how to manage my emotions. I learned how to "shutteth uppeth" around those who are older and wiser than I am. I learned how to bring a younger woman alongside me to give her the encouragement and wisdom she needs. I learned how to roast a turkey (even though I still think it's pretty gross having to butter the inside of a slimy bird . . . yuck!).

I learned how to do all of these things from Holly. Her mark on my life is undeniable, and her investment is one for which I will be eternally grateful!

The truth is, I'm still learning! We all are! But now it's time for me to put on the "older woman hat" and pay it forward—to share with you the wisdom that has been given to me over the years! Navigating life as a young woman can be tricky, but it doesn't need to be confusing or heartbreaking!

With some wisdom, you can navigate these years with dignity and grace, purpose and laughter! The decisions you make now can catapult you straight into your destiny! My prayer is that as you read each chapter, you will make choices that position you for the life you've dreamed of—one that makes heaven proud!

XOXO . . . NICOLE

1

Why Am I Here?

HOW TO DISCOVER YOUR GOD-GIVEN PURPOSE

Purpose is the place where your deep gladness meets the world's needs.

FREDERICK BUECHNER

You are not an accident. Maybe your parents told you that you were unwanted—that you were a mistake. They were wrong. You are more than an unwanted pregnancy. You are more than the result of two people having too much to drink and listening to too much Marvin Gaye one night.

I'm not sure if anyone has ever told you this before . . . but God created YOU for His great purposes! He has wonderful plans for you!

You are the loved-beyond-measure daughter of the King! You belong to God. You are His very own, created by Him and fashioned for greatness!

He could have plucked you out of eternity and placed you on earth at any point in history, but He chose you for now! He destined you to make an eternal difference on the planet at this very moment in time!

He has given you unique gifts and abilities, and wired you with a one-of-a-kind personality! He made you specifically to be in relationship with Him, and to discover the great plans He prepared for you before the foundations of the world were laid!

CREATED ON PURPOSE

Oh yes, you shaped me first inside, then out;
you formed me in my mother's womb.
I thank you, High God—you're breathtaking!
Body and soul, I am marvelously made!
I worship in adoration—what a creation!
You know me inside and out,
you know every bone in my body;
You know exactly how I was made, bit by bit,
how I was sculpted from

nothing into something.
Like an open book, you watched me
grow from conception to birth;
all the stages of my life were
spread out before you,
The days of my life all prepared
before I'd even lived one day.

PSALM 139:13-16, THE MESSAGE

This chapter is all about discovering God's unique purposes for your life. Our hope and prayer is that as you read, you will realize how very special you are, and how you can make a difference in the world around you!

RUN IN YOUR LANE

One thing I've noticed about sprinters is that each of them must run in his or her own lane. In fact, sprinters are disqualified if they decide to try to run in someone else's lane. Yet I wonder, *How many of us are trying to get through life running in someone else's lane?* We are all supposed to do great things on the earth. Each of us is given different gifts and different tools with which to do these great things.

You were gifted and called by God to run in the lane that He set before you . . . not in my lane or anyone else's. Your gifts and talents won't help me to fulfill my purpose (other than by being an inspiration to me) . . . and my gifts and talents won't help you to fulfill yours.

I really love to sing. Unfortunately, no one (other than God ☻) really wants to hear me. There were times when I was convinced that God had made a mistake, and I was supposed to be a singer . . . and so I wasted many hours pursuing something that wasn't mine to have. I was looking at all the lovely singer chicks, and I wanted to run in their lane.

I was so busy trying to run in someone else's lane that I wasn't focusing on figuring out what God had called me to do. What is the purpose for which I am here?

We often spend irreplaceable time desiring what another woman has. It is because we misunderstand our own value that we find ourselves coveting someone else's. Oprah gives us a great reminder about the treasure inside of us: "You have a gift that only you can give the world—that's the whole reason you're on the planet. Use your precious energy to build a magnificent life that really is attainable. The miracle of your existence calls for celebration every day."

It is good to be inspired by other runners, but remember to keep focused on the reason God created you. Dr. Martin Luther King, Jr., said, "Everyone has the power for greatness, not for fame but greatness, because greatness is determined by service." You are God's chosen servant. It is your job to begin the adventure of figuring out in just what area you are meant to serve.

IT'S NOT ALL ABOUT YOU!

Okay, I guess that's not entirely true. Jesus is madly and deeply in love with you! So much so that He willingly gave His life on the cross and rose from the dead just so that you and He could have a real, wonderful relationship for all eternity! If you were the only person on the whole planet, He would still have willingly sacrificed His life for YOU. So when it comes to Jesus' pursuit . . . IT IS ALL ABOUT YOU!

As we discover this incredible life-altering love that only Jesus can give, a revolutionary thing takes place in our souls. We begin to realize that because we are such a high priority in God's eyes, we don't have to make ourselves the highest priority in our own eyes any longer. In fact, as we experience more and more of the love of God, we are challenged to pass that same love on to others.

We begin to see that there are hurting people all around us—people who need Jesus, and who may only experience His love through our actions. As our eyes open to the needs all around us, we discover that life isn't all about getting our needs met—it's about how we can help and serve those in our world!

I (Nicole) awakened to this God-given purpose to serve others when I first moved to Los Angeles, straight out of high school. I had a dream in my heart—a BIG dream. Perhaps you do too. My dream was to be the next Sandra Bullock of the big screen! I was going to become a famous actress, and the applause and fame that came with that achievement would provide once and for all the validation I was desperately seeking. I prayed for God's favor and blessing as I went on auditions, and I practiced my Oscar acceptance speech—including a shout-out to Jesus . . . That's how I thought I would "give back" to Jesus after He endorsed the dreams of my heart.

There was only one problem with my grand ambitions . . . They were entirely self-focused.

My dreams were all about me! They were about the standing ovations I would receive, the fame I would gain, the money I would make, and the happiness I would experience.

Well, Jesus had different plans for my life . . . and I am glad He led me to discover His much better (in fact, PERFECT) plans for me! I began volunteering at my local church, and as I served people around me by making photocopies in the offices or praying with junior high girls at our youth services, my heart began to change. God showed me that a life of significance isn't a self-centered life where all my dreams come true exactly the way I want them to. Instead, God was calling me to a much larger life of generosity toward others.

I have now been on staff at Oasis Church for close to 10 years, and I have discovered a call to ministry and helping people that I never imagined possible! I truly love the life that God has given me, and I am honored that I get to serve and love people in the name of Jesus. I am so thankful that Jesus has led me to a life that reaches beyond myself—a life that by the grace of God gets to make an eternal impact on the lives of others!

I don't know what dreams you have for your life—your sights may be set on business, or the entertainment industry, or any number of other arenas—but I do know that as you follow Jesus, you will discover more and more how God can use you to reach out to others with the love that He has showered on you!

TEN WAYS TO REACH OUT

1. **Join your local church outreach to the community.** Find out what your local church is doing to make a difference in the community, and get involved! Whether it's participating in a neighborhood cleanup or giving away groceries to low-income families or something else, make sure you partner with your church to be

the hands and feet of Jesus to the impoverished and hurting in your very own community!

2. **Sponsor a child.** Help a child in a developing nation receive food, medical attention and education simply by making a monthly donation. When children are given opportunities for transformed lives, they will ultimately transform their communities. For more information, visit www.compassion.com.

3. **Invite a friend to church.** Inviting your friends to church is a great way to give them the greatest gift of all—an opportunity to hear about Jesus and the amazing gift of salvation we receive through faith in Him. Thom Rainer, when interviewing the "un-churched," found that 82 percent of those he talked to were "at least 'somewhat likely' to attend church if they are invited."[1] That's 8 out of 10. So go ahead and make the BIG ASK. You may be surprised at how one invitation changes a life!

4. **Mentor a younger woman.** You may not think you are OLD, but you are an older woman to someone! ☻ Take the time to invest in a younger woman who could use some love and encouragement from an

OLDER woman like you! Be her friend, her cheerleader, and an example of what a passionate follower of Jesus looks like! Just be real. You don't have to have all the answers to make a difference in a young woman's life; you just have to be someone who believes in her. Grab a coffee together, serve at your local church together, invite her over to have dinner with your family . . . and have fun swapping stories and chatting about God, friends, school, work, guys, and everything else that has a way of coming up when we women get to talking!

5. **Serve on a volunteer team in your local church.** Don't be content to sit on the bleachers as a spectator; get in the game! Find a team that interests you and begin serving! By being a contributor in your church, you'll truly experience what it means to be used by God in surprising and life-changing ways as you serve those around you.

6. **Tutor a student.** Every 26 seconds in America, a teenager drops out of high school.[2] You can help change that statistic by tutoring a student. Perhaps your few hours a week can help provide a young person with an academic future that would otherwise be impossible—an academic future that will make their dreams a reality.

7. **Come alongside a single parent.** It is estimated that half of all children in the United States will live in a single-parent home at some point during their childhoods.[3] Single mothers and fathers are truly in need of our support to help raise and care for their families. Why not offer to babysit once a month or run an errand or two for a single parent in your church or neighborhood? You can also call from time to time just to let them know you care.

8. **Bake cookies for your local police or fire department.** Let these brave men and women know you appreciate their efforts to protect your city, and honor their courage and commitment in the community. A small gesture goes a long way and reminds our local heroes that their service does not go unnoticed!

9. **Travel on an international missions trip with your local church.** Many churches partner with communities and nonprofits around the globe to make a difference. Learn more from your church about opportunities to travel internationally to bring love and hope to those in a different part of the world.

10. Build a water well with a group of friends. Nearly one billion people in the world don't have access to clean drinking water, which leads to illness, disease and premature death.[4] Rally your friends and come up with creative ways to raise the finances needed (just a few thousand dollars) to give a community access to clean drinking water. For more information, visit www.generositywater.com.

GET IN THE GAME!

I (Nicole) recently went to a girls' high school basketball game to support my friend, Paris. She totally dominated and kicked butt—I was so proud!

On my way to her game, I thought I was putting in a significant amount of effort to support my friend. I rearranged my schedule and drove out of my way in Los Angeles traffic. (If you've ever driven on the 405, you know this is a pretty big deal.) I even skipped dinner in order to make the game.

I was patting myself on the back for being such a good friend. After all, I had contributed a good amount of work—or so I thought until I started watching Paris and her team play . . .

Talk about hard work!

The players were the ones running up and down the basketball court, blocking shots and throwing passes. They were sweating and taking hits and going head-to-head with a tough team.

All I did was sit there and cheer my friend on. I didn't sweat. I didn't run. I just sat on the sidelines, watching.

As the game progressed, it became more and more apparent to me that Paris was a team player, while I was just a spectator.

When it comes to your involvement in the local church, God purposed you to be a team player, not a spectator. Your church needs YOU to get up from the stands and get in the game—because this "game" is of far more importance than any sporting event, no matter how loyal a fan you are of a sport.

Trophies and paychecks aren't on the line here—people and their eternal destinations are.

Admittedly, especially by the time the third or fourth quarter rolls around, life in the stands is way easier than life on the court. But there is no glory in the stands. There's no significance in the stands. Nothing heroic happens in the stands.

You only get to experience the kind of living that really matters by playing in the game. In your local church, playing in the game looks like contributing and serving! That's your opportunity to get involved and make an eternal impact for God's kingdom! God has given you unique gifts and talents that were meant to build the local church and impact the lives of other people!

Do you like teaching children? Can you play an instrument? Do you enjoy opening your home and hosting parties? Do you love creating spreadsheets? Are you skilled at working with your hands? Do you have a passion to reach teenagers with the message of Jesus?

Whatever your gifts and passions are, God Himself gave them to you for the purpose of making a difference in your local church! Don't put it off! Make the decision to do more than attend services. Explore God's purpose for your life by finding ways to serve! You may just discover passions and develop abilities you never knew you had!

WHAT'S YOUR STORY?

If you had to sum up your life story in three minutes, what would you say???

I (Nicole) was recently asked to do that in front of an audience, and I chose to share parts of my story I don't always mention when I speak. I talked about growing up in a home where my family had to overcome a number of challenges. I talked about my decision to begin following Jesus when I was 12 years old. I talked about moving to Los Angeles after high school, and about finding my church home at Oasis. I talked about how, by being committed to my local church, I have been able to discover God's will for my life and grow in my abilities as a leader and my character as a Jesus follower.

Some parts of my story are easy to talk about; in fact, it's fun to talk about them! We all have parts like that—chapters of our stories that involve great memories of love, acceptance, victory or accomplishment. These are the parts that are filled with laughter, smiles and inspiration.

Then there are the chapters we'd rather not talk about . . .

Some parts of our stories seem too painful to talk about. There may be things we have never told a single soul. We're afraid of what people might think or do. We are too ashamed or wounded to talk about these things.

Or maybe there are parts of our stories that are just a little embarrassing. These are the moments we look back on and ask, "What was I thinking?!"

What was I thinking . . . dating that person?

What was I thinking . . . hanging out with those guys?

What was I thinking . . . spending all that money I didn't have?

What was I thinking . . . getting that ridiculous haircut? ☻

When we think about these parts of our stories, we have to remember that God is good, and He doesn't cause bad things to happen to us. We should also keep in mind that God wants to take those parts of our stories that didn't turn out the way we wish they had and make something truly beautiful out of them.

We have a friend who grew up in church and had a strong relationship with Jesus when she was a little girl. However, as an adolescent and young adult, she walked away from her relationship with Jesus, hurt and disillusioned by abuses she had experienced in her past. She spent most of her twenties in nightclubs, addicted to drugs and alcohol. She moved from one bad relationship to the next. Then, in her late twenties, she encountered the presence of God in a radical way—in the bathroom of a Las Vegas nightclub, of all places! She left the partying life she knew and began coming back to church, where she rediscovered her relationship with Jesus. Over the next few years, God brought healing and restoration to the places of her heart that had been broken by the wounds of her past!

For a long time, our friend struggled with the idea of having to share her story with others. She was embarrassed and ashamed that she had walked away from the faith she had as a child and, in her words, "wasted" close to a decade of her life in a destructive lifestyle. But as she continued to grow in her faith, and with the support of her friends at church, she began to share with other young women the story of God's redemption in her life.

When she finally shared her story, she realized just how powerful a tool it was in God's kingdom! Women began to feel comfortable enough to share their own stories of abuse and brokenness, and her testimony played a key role in helping them find healing and hope in Jesus.

Today, she shares her story and offers hope to young women in group homes. Many of these teens are experiencing the radical transformation only Jesus can bring . . . all because our friend had enough courage to share her story!

Whatever your story is . . . please know that it is a powerful tool in God's hands. When we have the courage to share our stories, we create opportunities for others to experience the same freedom and hope we have found in Jesus. God wants to use every part of your story (the good, the bad, and everything in between) for His great purpose and plan!

FIVE QUESTIONS TO ASK BEFORE MAKING A BIG DECISION

The decisions we make matter. They lead us either toward or farther away from God's purpose and destiny for our lives. With every choice—BIG or SMALL—that we make, we have an opportunity to become more like Jesus and walk in His will for our lives. Whether it's a decision about what school to apply to, or what city to move to, or whom to date, or what local church to be a part of, or whether or not to have that difficult conversation with a friend . . . we need to rely on more than our own experiences and perspectives! The great news is that we don't have to make these decisions by ourselves! God generously offers His wisdom for every area of our lives!

In the book of James, the Bible teaches us: "If any of you is deficient in wisdom, let him ask of the giving God [Who gives] to everyone liberally and ungrudgingly, without reproaching or faultfinding, and it will be given him" (Jas. 1:5, AMP).

God has wisdom for you! You don't have to go through life guessing and hoping things will turn out okay. You can rely on God's direction and guidance for your life! Below are five simple questions that will help you unlock divine wisdom for your life in your decision-making:

1. **What does the Bible have to say about the decision I am considering making?** The Bible provides much-needed direction for our lives. It's like our spiritual GPS! God speaks to us and gives us the guidance we need to make choices that will lead us to His perfect will. (Tip for free: Find more than one passage or Bible verse to help you navigate your current situation. The more Bible verses you consider, the more likely you are to accurately interpret the direction God is giving you through His Word.)

2. **Have I talked this over with the right people?** Discuss the decision you have to make—BEFORE you make it—with people you can trust. Make sure to get advice from people who are spiritually mature and have wisdom to offer in the area you are making a decision about! Get counsel from people who are further along in the journey than you are and who can actually give you great, godly advice. Be open-minded as you discuss your options with pastors and mentors.

3. **When I pray, how is the Holy Spirit confirming direction found in the Bible?** Take time to pray and ask God what you should or shouldn't do. When we pray, we should ask for God's perfect will to be done in our lives . . . and that He would show us what that looks like in our current decision-making. Then, we need to *listen*. Prayer is a process of listening and reflecting as much as it is a time of talking. Through faith in Jesus, we have been given access to the Spirit of God, who speaks to us and gives us guidance in our lives! (Tip for free: The Holy Spirit will never lead us to do something contrary to the direction for our lives found in the Bible. If you believe God is leading you in a specific direction, make sure it's consistent with the guidance found in your Bible.)

4. **Does this choice benefit others and the local church?** Take a minute to consider how your decision will affect the lives of those around you. Is the decision you are about to make going to build the local church and make a positive impact on the lives of other people?

5. **What is the honorable thing to do?** Don't just make the easy and convenient choice. Make the decision that honors Jesus and brings glory to Him. That might mean choosing something that is inconvenient or that requires sacrifice . . . but in the end, it will be worth it! Great lives are built on decisions made with eternity in mind, not just what makes sense in the here and now!

FAST FORWARD, PLEASE!

None of us likes to wait. Is there anything more annoying than sitting in a waiting room??? We even give up on a new television show if the plot isn't developing fast enough. Have you ever switched in and out of lanes just to move two cars ahead of the person in the "slower lane"? Or decided to come back to a store later rather than wait in a line with more than four people in it?? Surely we aren't the only two people who do these things . . .

Our "let's-keep-things-moving" attitude has its perks. We can pack a lot of productive activities into one day. We can check off an impressive number of tasks on a to-do list. Tight deadlines inject a weird adrenaline-rush into our workday. We keep our friends and families on their toes with our ever-evolving interests. ☻

But when it comes to fulfilling purpose and destiny, there are just some things (LIKE CHARACTER) that refuse to be put on the fast track.

If our lives were movies, we would prefer to fast-forward through certain parts—mainly the ones where we feel like we're just waiting for the action to heat up. Can we skip the opening credits, the slow-paced back story, and the monotonous "getting-to-know-the-characters" dialogue, so we can get to the good stuff—like the car chase and the explosions and the showdown between the good guy and the bad guy, ultimately ending with the leading love interests defeating the odds and living happily ever after?

(Yes, I am aware that if there were a movie made of my life, it probably wouldn't include a car chase or an explosion, but you get the idea!)

We all wish we had that real-life fast-forward button. We wish we could fast-forward through college and just get handed that degree already! We wish we could fast-forward through the under-paid, crazy-hours job to get that corner office. We wish we could fast-forward past our singleness and press play on our wedding day. We wish we could fast-forward through the challenges in our marriage or family and get to the good stuff—the stuff famous authors write relationship and parenting books about. We wish we could fast-forward the healing process of our soul and restart at the place where we have overcome the hurts and disappointments of our past.

But then I remember King David from the Bible.

Think about David, exiled from Israel even though he was anointed to be the next king. Out of jealousy and insecurity, King Saul plotted to kill poor David. David was forced out of his home, lived in enemy territory, posed as a mental patient, hid out in caves, and was surrounded by disgruntled men who at one point wanted to stone him. He was misunderstood, persecuted and lied about . . . and he hadn't done anything to deserve it.

Glimmers of a great king shone through during these hard times. David became disciplined. He became wise. He became generous. He became forgiving. He became compassionate. He became strong. There were things being forged inside of David in those caves, in the midst of exile. While King Saul was seeking to kill David, God was seeking to make a king out of David.

And God did just that. He used the caves. He used the exile. He used enemy ground. He used disgruntled men. He used a mad and jealous king. Somehow, God was able to take what was meant to destroy David and use it as a tool to bring about transformation in David's soul.

Weapons of destruction, when placed in God's hands, have a way of becoming weapons of divine purpose.

Perhaps the very things we are in such a hurry to fast-forward through are the very things that make us . . . make us more Christlike, make us more compassionate. Make us stronger. Make us purpose-minded. Make us wiser. Make us more obedient. More willing. More Kingdom-minded.

So the next time we feel the need to try to push the fast-forward button by pleading with God in prayer, or fantasizing about quitting or escaping our responsibilities, or throwing a pity party . . . why not first ask ourselves:

What is God up to in this moment of my life? What is He developing in my character as part of the divine purpose He has for me? How is He *preparing me* for what He has already *prepared for me*?

For we are God's [own] handiwork (His workmanship), recreated in Christ Jesus, [born anew] that we may do those good works which God predestined (planned beforehand) for us [taking paths which He prepared ahead of time], that we should walk in them [living the good life which He prearranged and made ready for us to live].

EPHESIANS 2:10, AMP

MORE, PLEASE!

(Additional reading)

The Purpose Driven Life by Rick Warren

Warrior Chicks by Holly Wagner

Enjoying Where You Are on the Way to Where You Are Going by Joyce Meyer

Stop Acting Like a Christian, Just Be One by Christine Caine

Weird by Craig Groeschel

2

One of a Kind

HOW TO CELEBRATE YOUR UNIQUE STYLE

Today you are You,
that is truer than true.
There is no one alive
who is Youer than You.

DR. SEUSS

In all of time, there will never be another you. No one else will ever have your DNA, your fingerprints, your destiny . . . or your style. ☻

Before we get into celebrating our own unique styles, it might be good to reshape our minds and hearts about what is beautiful. In our society, beauty is often misunderstood. Sometimes, when I see *People* magazine's "50 Most Beautiful People," I wonder, *Says who? And how come? Who picks and decides what's beautiful?*

I've read articles about women in other countries wearing shoes that are too small in order to make their feet smaller, or having surgeries that lighten their skin. We live in Southern California, where you can have something augmented on every street corner. There is nothing wrong with fixing something you want fixed . . . but you need to understand that changing something on the outside won't change what is inside.

The truth is, we are all created with intention—intricately woven in our mother's wombs (see Ps. 139)—and Genesis 1 tells us that everything God makes is good. If that's true, then we do not have to yield ourselves to media's standard of beauty. We are simply responsible to be our best selves in every area of our lives.

As women, we can be pretty hard on ourselves—and because we're hard on ourselves, we're also hard on each other. Jealousy and judgment can fuel and color our relationships if we're not careful to love what God has given us and appreciate the differences around us. When we truly love ourselves, we can celebrate all kinds of women in our world rather than waste time judging and competing with them.

Jealousy is a wasted emotion . . . and we all face it and have to deal with it in our own hearts. Honestly, how many times has jealousy actually been beneficial to our lives? Jealousy and unhealthy competition hinder relationships and feed insecurity.

When we see a friend who has a pair of shoes or a purse we can't afford, or a new hairstyle we could never pull off, how do we respond? Do we get excited and celebrate with them, or do we become critical and find it impossible to give a compliment? What about those moments at the gym (or flipping through a magazine) when we wish we had someone else's body parts or hair or lips or whatever else we feel insecure about?

One of the hardest jealousy tests is opportunity. When our friends or people we know have opportunities we don't have, how do we respond? A friend gets a boyfriend . . . Someone else gets the promotion we wanted at work . . . At Christmas, everyone except us gets the clothes and shoes we had on our lists.

The thing is . . . what other people have is not the real problem. We need to commit to cultivating gratitude in our hearts for what we do have.

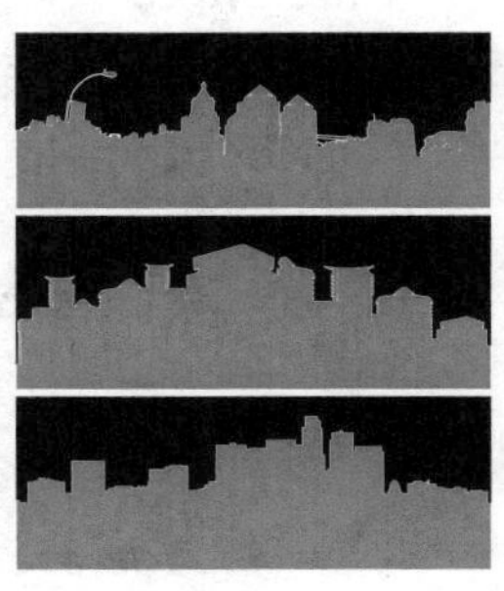

Judgment is another wasted emotion. We all come in different colors, shapes and sizes. We live in different cities, cultures and economic brackets. Because our world conditions us to think a certain way about beauty and style, we make judgments against others without considering the context of their lives.

Have you ever been at school or work or Starbucks . . . and thought to yourself as you looked at someone, *Whoa! Shoulda never left the house like that!* Well, maybe she's a new mom, and because she's breastfeeding every two hours, she hasn't had a shower in two days, much less had time to do her hair (been there!).

Don't we all have a photo (or 2 . . . or 10!) from our pasts that we hope no one ever sees? Some of my (Holly's) outfits from the '80s are scary . . . not to mention the big bangs!

Let's be the kind of women who aren't critics of other women. We don't have to be judgmental—we can give people grace. Let's be the kind of women who aren't overwhelmed with jealousy, but are learning to love and see ourselves the way God loves and sees us.

How we navigate jealousy and judgment determines the way we celebrate. Until we can celebrate what we have and who we are, we can't appreciate our own unique styles . . . or the unique styles of others.

Now, to help you celebrate yourself, here are . . .

TEN THINGS GOD THINKS ABOUT YOU

1. **You are one of a kind.**

   "I will confess and praise You for You are fearful and wonderful and for the awful wonder of my birth! Wonderful are Your works, and that my inner self knows right well" (Ps. 139:14, AMP).

"You are altogether beautiful, my darling, beautiful in every way" (Song of Sol. 4:7, NLT).

2. **You are loved completely.**

"'Though the mountains be shaken and the hills be removed, yet my unfailing love for you will not be shaken nor my covenant of peace be removed,' says the LORD, who has compassion on you" (Isa. 54:10).

"The LORD appeared to us in the past, saying: 'I have loved you with an everlasting love; I have drawn you with loving-kindness'" (Jer. 31:3).

"Neither height nor depth, nor anything else in all creation, will be able to separate us from the love of God that is in Christ Jesus our Lord" (Rom. 8:39).

3. **You are a treasure.**

"She is far more precious than jewels and her value is far above rubies or pearls" (Prov. 31:10, AMP).

"The LORD has declared today that you are his people, his own special treasure, just as he promised, and that you must obey all his commands" (Deut. 26:18, NLT).

4. **You are purposed.**

"'For I know the plans I have for you,' declares the Lord, 'plans to prosper you and not to harm you, plans to give you hope and a future'" (Jer. 29:11).

"The Lord will fulfill his purpose for me; your love, O Lord, endures forever—do not abandon the works of your hands" (Ps. 138:8).

"For we are His workmanship, created in Christ Jesus for good works, which God prepared beforehand that we should walk in them" (Eph. 2:10, NKJV).

5. **You are a new creation.**

"Therefore, if anyone is in Christ, [she] is a new creation; the old has gone, the new has come!" (2 Cor. 5:17).

"Instead, let the Spirit renew your thoughts and attitudes. Put on your new nature, created to be like God—truly righteous and holy" (Eph. 4:23-24, NLT)

6. **You are in right standing with God.**

We often hear the word "righteous" in church. Just in case you aren't sure what that means, it simply means that you are in right standing with God through Christ. In other words, God's not mad at you—He loves you, believes in you, and has purposefully placed you on this earth.

"God is all mercy and grace—not quick to anger, is rich in love" (Ps. 145:8, THE MESSAGE).

"If we admit our sins—make a clean breast of them—he won't let us down; he'll be true to himself. He'll forgive our sins and purge us of all wrongdoing" (1 John 1:9-10, THE MESSAGE).

"But I, yes I, am the one who takes care of your sins—that's what I do. I don't keep a list of your sins" (Isa. 43:25, THE MESSAGE).

7. **You have been set free to set others free.**

You have a story to tell. Don't be afraid to share it.

"The Spirit of the Sovereign Lord is upon me, for the Lord has anointed me to bring good news to the poor. He has sent me to comfort the brokenhearted and to proclaim that captives will be released and prisoners will be freed" (Isa. 61:1, NLT).

"God is our refuge and strength, an ever-present help in trouble. Therefore we will not fear, though the earth give way and the mountains fall into the heart of the sea, though its waters roar and foam and the mountains quake with their surging" (Ps. 46:1-3).

"For God has not given us a spirit of fear, but of power and of love and of a sound mind" (2 Tim. 1:7, NKJV).

"There is no fear in love; but perfect love casts out fear, because fear involves torment" (1 John 4:18, NKJV).

"So do not fear, for I am with you; do not be dismayed, for I am your God. I will strengthen you and help you; I will uphold you with my righteous right hand" (Isa. 41:10).

8. **You were created for family.**

"Even if my father and mother abandon me, the Lord will hold me close" (Ps. 27:10, NLT).

"Father to the fatherless, defender of widows—this is God, whose dwelling is holy. God places the lonely in families; he sets the prisoners free and gives them joy" (Ps. 68:5-6, NLT).

"So you have not received a spirit that makes you fearful slaves. Instead, you received God's Spirit when he adopted you as his own children. Now we call him, 'Abba, Father' [Daddy God]" (Rom. 8:15, NLT).

9. You have a place in the kingdom of God.

"How lovely is your dwelling place, O LORD of Heaven's Armies.
I long, yes, I faint with longing to enter the courts of the LORD.
With my whole being, body and soul, I will shout joyfully to the living God.
Even the sparrow finds a home, and the swallow builds her nest and raises her young
at a place near your altar, O LORD of Heaven's Armies, my King and my God!
What joy for those who can live in your house, always singing your praises.
What joy for those whose strength comes from the LORD, who have set their minds on a pilgrimage to Jerusalem.
When they walk through the Valley of Weeping, it will become a place of refreshing springs. The autumn rains will clothe it with blessings.
They will continue to grow stronger and each of them will appear before God in Jerusalem" (Ps. 84:1-7, NLT).

10. You have a legacy to leave.

"We will not hide these truths from our children; we will tell the next generation about the glorious deeds of the Lord, about his power and his mighty wonders" (Ps. 78:4, NLT).

"A good man leaves an inheritance [of moral stability and goodness] to his children's children, and the wealth of the sinner [finds its way eventually] into the hands of the righteous, for whom it was laid up" (Prov. 13:22, AMP).

Now that you know what God thinks about you, we're going to dive into discovering and celebrating your own unique style. We don't know everything, and we certainly are not the style experts, but because we've made a few bad fashion choices in the past, we've learned what's best for our unique selves . . . and hope we can help you too!

Let's start with hair . . .

THE RIGHT HAIRCUT FOR YOUR FACE

We've occasionally missed the mark, so we called in some help from hairstylists in Los Angeles. According to the experts we talked to, it is better to play up what God gave you than to go totally into left field (turns out this is true in every area of style).

We all look through magazines . . . or watch movies and see women with great haircuts. Then we go to our hairdressers and tell them that we want that haircut. If it's not a good choice, let's hope our hairdressers are honest enough to say, "That one doesn't suit the shape of your face." If it is a good match, they begin cutting away, and we get ready to enjoy our fun new look!

But not every hairdresser is going to tell us the truth. So how do we determine if Beyonce's color or Ginnifer Goodwin's pixie cut would work for us?

Listen, the great thing about hair is that it grows! Oftentimes you won't know if something works until you try it. So we should all feel the freedom to try new things! We want to share what we have learned so you can play away!

It's good to start by considering what will accentuate the strengths of your face. (For instance, if you have big, beautiful eyes, then the cut you choose should highlight them.)

SHAPE

If your gorgeous head is long and square, then longer hair is the most flattering. If your cute face is narrow, then layers will make the hair appear fuller and look great around your face. If your lovely face is round, a cut above the chin line or way beneath it will be the most flattering.

If you have a large forehead, it's good to have some sort of bangs to soften the outline of your face. If you have a tiny forehead, bangs may not be the best look.

   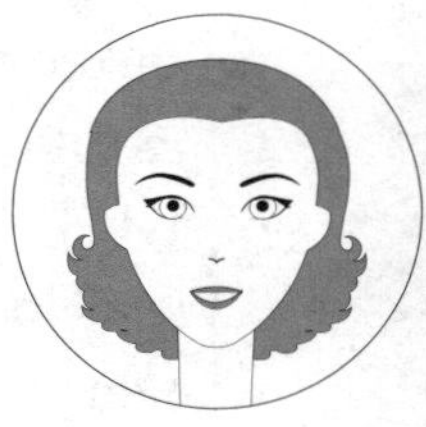

COLOR

Use color to accent great traits on your face. We found a little help online for this one.[1]

YOUR EYE / SKIN COLOR	YOUR HAIR COLOR
Light Eye Color: Light Skin	Keep your color light and fair with your hair depth
Light Eye Color: Medium Skin	Keep your color light to medium depth
Light Eye Color: Dark Skin	Anything goes
Medium Eye Color: Light Skin	Keep your color light to medium depth
Medium Eye Color: Medium Skin	Keep your color light to medium depth

Medium Eye Color: Dark Skin	Keep your color dark to medium depth
Dark Eye Color: Light Skin	Anything goes
Dark Eye Color: Medium Skin	Keep your color medium to dark depth
Dark Eye Color: Dark Skin	Keep your color a deeper depth

Remember, unhealthy hair is not attractive, so while playing with colors, do the work of keeping your hair healthy so you can look your best.

EIGHT TIPS FOR HEALTHY HAIR

1. We should wash our hair every other day . . . or every three days. Three days is better, but if you have oily hair, stick with every other day.

2. Never, ever put conditioner on your roots. That clogs up hair follicles, makes hair oilier sooner, and can cause dandruff from build-up on your scalp.

3. For short hair, conditioner goes on the ends of the hair; for long hair, apply conditioner from the nape of the neck down.

4. When it comes to ponytails, tight holders can damage hair, so try a cloth ponytail holder or a fabric-covered elastic band.

5. To keep hair healthy, getting it trimmed every 8 to 10 weeks is a good idea.

6. The right brush is important. Try a natural fiber brush, like boar bristle, because the bristle will bend before your hair breaks. A plastic bristle is not as forgiving and can lead to breakage.

7. The safest time to comb or brush hair is when it's totally wet or dry. Hair is most fragile when it's in between wet and dry.

8. The less heat the better. All heat will do some damage. Keep the hair dryer at least an inch from the hair, and try not to flatiron your hair everyday—that will lead to breaks and split ends.

MAKEUP AND GROOMING

Day or night, makeup is a tool to highlight our features and help us look as fresh-faced as possible. Here are some helpful items to keep in your beauty box at all times (good to carry an extra set in your purse also):

- **Foundation:** Mineral powders are a great way to blend foundation and powder while creating a very natural look.

- **Blush and Bronzer:** Find a blush that makes you glow. Bronzer (in the right color for your skin) also does a great job of adding color without overdoing it. Apply a little more for a night on the town than you would for the office.

- **Lip Gloss/Lipstick:** Fun fact to help with purchasing lip gloss or lipstick—turn your hand over. Look at the backside of your pinky finger. This is basically the color of your lips . . . so when you're looking at lip products in your favorite store, use your pinky to find a match. By the way . . . did you know that the average woman ingests about 52 tubes of lipstick in her lifetime? Might want to purchase organic . . .

- **Mascara:** Mascara helps us look vibrant by bringing out our eyes. Choose a black or nearly black mascara (dark brown is great for very fair skin and/or very light hair) and a wand that will thicken lashes without clumping. During the day, try two coats; at night, try three or four for glamour.

- **Eyeliner/Eye Shadow:** Feel free to use eyeliner to enhance eyes—just not too thick or too much. Blend it for a smoky eye, or draw a thinner line above the lash line and on the lower lash line . . . and then apply eye shadow. Eye shadow is an enhancer. In your twenties, you can play around with color a little more—green, purple, gold or other shades applied in a subtle, classy way works for you. After 30, neutrals that vary in depth (light brown to chocolate brown, grey to charcoal, and so forth) are best.

Makeup works best on a clean face. You don't have to buy extremely expensive brands to take care of your skin—there are great products at your local drugstore. Wash your face at night before sleeping and apply a moisturizer or night cream. When you're rising and shining . . . wash your face again. Try a toner and then a moisturizer with sunscreen (very important, no matter your skin color!).

Did you know that your skin is your body's biggest organ? That basically means that whatever you put on your skin . . . you might as well be eating! Try to choose products that are organic or natural—read the labels and try especially to avoid mineral oil and parabens (all those words that end with yl—methyl, propyl, butyl, and so on).

Now, some basic grooming tips:

- **Plucking Eyebrows:** Groomed eyebrows frame the eyes and can help transform our faces. You can pluck at home, if you know what you're doing . . . or leave the fun to a professional! Don't be afraid to remove any other hair (for instance, above the lip or on the chin) to show off your gorgeous face.

- **Shaved, Lotioned Skin:** Listen, I've never met a woman who enjoys shaving her legs. ☻ But, clean-shaven legs conditioned with moisturizer feel and look great. Also, apply lotion to your body after the shower—moisturized skin glows and feels smooth and clean. Remember to read your labels at the store!!

- **Basic Manicure and Pedicure:** Clean nails and cuticles go a long way in helping us look polished and put together. You don't have to get a manicure and pedicure every week—just keep a great top coat and a few colors you like at home to do your own nails. Use a good hand and foot cream to stay moisturized. If you bite your nails or cuticles . . . STOP! Aside from the sanitary reasons, it's just not attractive.

FIND THE PERFECT PAIR OF JEANS

Besides ending world hunger and human trafficking, there are few things more difficult than finding the perfect pair of jeans. Why does it always seem like the jeans we find fit great . . . in one body part only?

The bottom fits, but there's so much space at the waist; the waist and bottom fit, but the calves are so tight they feel like compression socks; they fit perfectly, except they're three inches too short.

We understand your frustration! How many pairs do we have to try before we find "the one"? But when we are finally standing in the dressing room in the perfect pair, rejoicing with all of heaven, all the frustration is worth it.

Body shape and height must be considered when jean shopping. We don't really like those articles in magazines that compare our bodies to types of fruit. Who wants to be called an apple or a pear? And what if you're neither? Still, we don't want to throw the baby out with the bath water, because there is some truth to those articles . . . (But don't worry, we're not gonna relate your gorgeous body to a piece of produce!)

- **Boot-cut/Flared Jeans:** This style accentuates curves and looks best on ladies with hips. The slight or full flare, starting at the knee, brings proportion to the body and looks great on tall women. On the flip side, this style can swallow up a petite body. Pair this style of jeans with shirts that are tucked in, or that extend just below the waistline. Pumps, boots (hidden under the flare) and flats all work with this style.

- **Wide-leg Jeans:** This style is great for work, especially in a dark rinse, because it looks so similar to trousers. For those with fuller hips and thighs, this style is extremely slimming; for those who are petite, this style also works when tailored to fit well. Pair this style with shirts that are tucked in (button-ups with a belt you like look great), tanks, or jackets and shirts that hang just past the waistline. Pumps (round, peep-toe or pointed), boots (hidden under the wide leg) and flats all work with this style.

- **Straight-leg Jeans:** This style is great for those of us who are apprehensive about skinny jeans, but love them anyway. Straight-leg jeans work for pretty much everyone, regardless of body type, and they look great on a lazy Saturday, a date night, or at the office. Pair this style with a wide variety of shirts—tucked in or just below the waistline, boyfriend jackets and longer shirts, shirtdresses or cardigans. Pumps, boots (over or under the straight leg), short boots and flats work great with this style.

- **Skinny Jeans:** This style works for any body type, when worn right. Whether you have curvy hips or no hips, slender legs or fuller legs, skinny jeans can work for you. Generally, stretchy skinny jeans tend to gather at the knee, squeeze too tight on the rear end or legs, or loosen after one wear. Still, for comfort in the waistline, we do suggest you try a skinny jean that has a little stretch. Pair this jean with almost any kind of shirt and jacket. If you have fuller thighs, try wearing a long shirt, cardigan, button-up or shirt-dress (play with belts, long necklaces and scarves) with your skinnies. When it comes to shoes, anything goes with skinny jeans—riding boots, cowboy boots, booties, pumps (any kind), stilettos (to keep the look modern, but classy, try not to get the platform too high) and even flats look great.

More thoughts on denim:

- **Low-Rise Denim:** Low-rise or even high-waisted denim must be worn with caution. Low-rise jeans especially can result in exposing what you don't want exposed! Generally, if you are blessed with a bottom, choose a jean that is higher in the back to avoid exposure.

- **Rear Pockets:** Décor on the rear pockets is pretty risky and will probably be in style for only a short period of time. We all want our rear ends to look good, but we probably don't need signs that point people to them. For the most flattering look, avoid pockets that are too tiny and those that come below the rear end onto the top of the thigh.

- **Distressed Denim:** Distressed denim detail can be very attractive—the jeans look worn-in and have an interesting look . . . lines that are faded, wiskering, holes, shredding, and so forth. Just make sure the lines are flattering, and the holes are not too revealing.

- **Best Rinse for My Body:** For the most part, medium to dark rinses are best, because they are the most versatile between home, work and social settings. Darker rinses are also the most flattering for every body type.

- **Length of Jeans:** This one can be tricky, especially if you are very tall or short. If you're wearing flats, you want denim that stops just below the top of the flat (or that can be cuffed). If you're wearing heels, the jeans should hang a quarter inch or less from the floor. Ankle-length jeans can also be great—just wear them well!

- **Don't Be Afraid to Tailor:** If you find jeans that fit perfectly, except they're too long or too short or the waist is a little too big, find a great tailor in your city and have those minor adjustments made. Don't be afraid to spend a little more for jeans that you'll wear—it's worth it!

TODAY'S IMPORTANT ACCESSORIES

Now it's time for the next topic to help you celebrate your unique style . . . accessories. We asked a Nordstrom buyer and a few of our friends what accessories they consider essential.

- **Large Pearl Studs:** Pearl studs are classic.

- **Diamond Studs:** Another classic choice.

- **Hoop Earrings:** Hoops work well with T-shirts and tanks, as well as business casual clothes. Hoops also look great with ponytails.
- **Gold Bracelets:** Try wearing a cuff, bangles, or a combination of chunky and skinny bracelets.
- **Silver bracelets:** As with gold, try wearing a cuff, bangles, or a combination of chunky and skinny bracelets.
- **Statement Necklace:** Try a necklace with large stones, or several short strands of pearls, or one necklace that looks like several necklaces in one.
- **Animal or Ethnic Scarf:** Try cheetah or leopard print, or something with a loud, fun color pattern that is flattering to your skin tone.
- **Statement Ring or Cocktail Ring:** This could be a family heirloom, or a ring with a large stone (like turquoise) or a collection of stones.
- **Camel Leather Purse:** This color goes with anything; it translates from day to night, casual to dressy; and it coordinates with outfits for work, home or social outings.
- **Vintage Earrings and Rhinestone Bracelet:** Timeless jewelry that looks great with a little black dress, at

a nice dinner or formal event, or on an interview. Beautiful jewelry is also fun with simple V-neck tees and that perfect pair of jeans.

- **Cognac Boots:** Cognac refers to the color of this leather boot. (The name is derived from brandy, a.k.a. cognac, which is amber in color and generally darkens with age.) Like camel, this color goes with everything and translates from day to night and casual to dressy.

- **Skinny Belt:** Skinny belts look great with jeans and a button-up, on a shirtdress, or over the waist of a cardigan and pencil skirt. Try a fun color like red, turquoise or yellow, or a pattern like cheetah.

FIVE VERSATILE MUST-HAVE SHOES

1. **Nude Pumps:** closed-toe pumps, closed-toe platform pumps, peep-toe stilettos . . .

2. **Black Pumps:** closed-toe stiletto, round-toe, thick-heel, pointed-toe . . .

3. **Flat Sandals**: gladiator, gold coach, simple brown . . .

4. **Boots**: riding boots, military-looking boot, cowboy boots . . .

5. **Wild Card:** the perfectly you shoe (fun flat, colorful sparkle shoe, turquoise wild shoe . . .)

UNDERGARMENTS

- **Really Great Bra:** Yes, we know how awkward it can be to be fitted for a bra . . . and yes, we know they can be expensive . . . but you should have at least one bra that fits you well. A bra that is not fitted can be uncomfortable or squeeze your back too tight. A bra that fits not only feels good, but also looks great under your clothes.

- **Strapless Bra in Black and Nude:** Call us old fashioned, but we believe that straps can ruin an outfit, so strapless dresses, racerback tanks, boatneck shirts and other odd-shaped, cute shirts should be worn over strapless bras. (If you need straps, try a bra with clear straps.)

- **Comfortable Pretty Panties:** Panties that are too tight, or too large, leave underwear lines that can be seen through our workout pants, our work slacks and even our jeans.

- **Undergarments in Nude, Black and Neutral Tones:** Undies can be any color you like; however, be sure to have some underwear in nude or neutral tones and in black, to wear under your nicer clothes, as well as your lighter colored pants and skirts (just don't wear black under those!!).

EIGHT ESSENTIAL ITEMS (A.K.A. WARDROBE EMERGENCY KIT)[2]

1. **A Full-length Mirror in a Well-lit Area:** Have you ever shopped in your favorite department store, stood in front of that cheeky little mirror under a sneaky little light, and purchased an outfit . . . only to get home and discover that the outfit looks nothing like it did in the store? Keep a great full-length mirror at home.

2. **A Lint Roller:** This is a necessity, especially if you have animals in the house. Synthetic fibers manage to catch every piece of hair, dirt and more.

3. **Fashion Tape:** Again, this may seem old fashioned, but bra straps can spoil a great dress, shirt or outfit. Fashion tape can help keep your button-ups from gaping open and your little black dress from revealing too much.

4. **Sewing Kit:** Believe me, sewing is not my specialty—or even my ability—but I cannot tell you how many times a button has fallen off my favorite jacket or button-up . . . Having extra buttons in the house helps!

5. **Tide® to Go Pen:** This little helper fits anywhere—in a purse, at home, in a drawer at the office . . . and it's perfect for dealing with something we spilled at lunch, or spit-up from our sweet babies (or our friends' babies!).

6. **Rescue Sponge:** Search online and order this little item to keep at home for removing makeup on the collar or deodorant on your shirt (how does that happen, anyway?!).

7. **Garment Bag:** Good bras and underwear (refer to our undergarment section) are not cheap. A garment bag will help you wash your bras and panties without them wrapping around other clothing items or the middle part of the washing machine. For longevity, use a garment bag (Woolite works great too).

8. **Feminine Products:** *Muy importante* for obvious reasons. ☻ Just keep a spare in your purse.

SWAP AND SHOP

We've learned a lot about finances as a church family, and there are plenty of resources to help you stick to a budget that lets you be smart with your cash flow and still do some shopping.

Some of the women we know host "Swap and Shop" parties. Each woman brings items from her closet—everything from purses to dresses to shoes—that are in great shape. Everything is laid out on the floor, like a living room boutique, and all the ladies shop . . . for free!

Try hosting a "Swap and Shop" party with your girlfriends. You'll have a chance to pick up some cool new items for your wardrobe without damaging your wallet.

We hope these little tips will help you on your style journey!

Remember, there will never be another you—you are one of a kind! Try making classic fashion and beauty choices, while adopting a few new trends each season, so that your style is simultaneously timeless and modern. The goal in celebrating your unique style is to enhance your natural beauty and make the most of what God gave you . . . and then have fun celebrating others by sharing what you've learned with all the fabulous women in your world!

MORE, PLEASE!

(Additional reading)

Can I Have And Do It All Please? by Christine Caine

The Lucky Guide to Mastering Any Style by Kim France and Andrea Linett

InStyle's *The New Secrets of Style*

Good Girls Don't Have to Dress Bad by Shari Braendel

A Jewel in His Crown by Priscilla Shirer

3

Healthy Living

HOW TO LIVE LONG AND LOOK GOOD

He who is loose and slack in his work is brother to him who is a destroyer and he who does not use his endeavors to heal himself is brother to him who commits suicide.

PROVERBS 18:9, AMP

The physical part of you is not some piece of property belonging to the spiritual part of you. God owns the whole works. So let people see God in and through your body.

1 CORINTHIANS 6:19-20, THE MESSAGE

As humans we are three-part beings.

Spirit. Soul. Body.

We often are better at feeding our spirits and nurturing our souls than we are at taking care of our bodies.

Each of us has been given only one body.

God has trusted us with that one amazing body to fulfill the purposes for which He created us.

I want to finish my race strong, so that means I need to do what I can to keep my body strong. I can't control the toxins in the environment, but for the most part, I can manage what I eat and how I treat my body.

Just like the verse in 1 Corinthians says: "God owns the whole works."

Our bodies are His, so let's do the best we can to take care of them!

Seven years ago, I (Holly) was diagnosed with breast cancer . . . and began my healing journey. I started studying and reading a lot about health, and I came to understand that I have an obligation to take care of the one and only body God has given me to fulfill my purpose on planet Earth. There are steps I can take to aid in the prevention of disease.

I really wish someone had told me these things when I was in my twenties or thirties. That might have spared me some of the challenges I faced. So maybe they will help you!

One thing I learned is that even though my doctors were great, I should never just yield my health care to them blindly. While they are certainly knowledgeable, doctors are not infallible . . . and neither is the U.S. Food and Drug Administration (FDA) or the American Medical Association (AMA).

For example, at one point in history, many doctors said that formula was better for the health of babies than breast milk was. They were wrong and have now acknowledged that breast milk is better. The FDA has approved drugs that caused so many problems they were later taken off the market.

These great organizations have made mistakes—they are not perfect. So it is okay for you to ask questions of your doctors. Do your own research.

I am not a doctor, so the things I share here came from my own research and reading. I hope my experience will encourage you to do some reading of your own, and then get busy building a strong and healthy body!!!

FIVE GOOD THINGS I EAT

1. **Organic Vegetables and Fruits.** I choose organic produce whenever possible, because so many pesticides are used in non-organic farming, and our bodies really are not designed to handle the amount of toxins thrown at us daily. I may not be able to do much about the pollutants in the air I breathe, but I can control what goes in my mouth. If you were to do just one thing to improve your health, I would tell you to eat four pieces of fresh fruit and two big raw salads full of vegetables each day.

2. **Whole Food Supplements.** Your body is deficient in vitamins, minerals, enzymes and cofactors. That is

a fact. There is no way you can get all the nutrients you need by eating food, because our soil is depleted of many of the nutrients it once had. There simply is no way you are getting the nutrients you need, unless you are supplementing your intake.

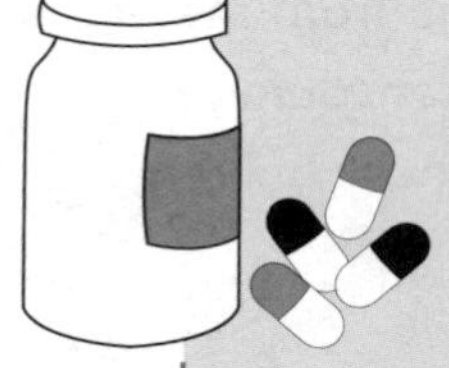

I take quite a few supplements—the whole-food kind (generally not the kind you can get at your corner drug store). You might want to consider taking some as well; however, please remember that vitamin supplements won't compensate for a poor diet. They are meant to help fill nutritional gaps in a good one.

3. **Goat's Milk Kefir or Yogurt.** Yep. Goat's milk. It might take you a minute or two to adjust to the taste, but then you will love it! It contains vitamins, minerals, electrolytes, trace elements, enzymes, protein and fatty acids that are utilized by your body with ease. In fact, your body can digest goat's milk in just 20 minutes. It takes 2 to 3 hours to digest cow's milk.

4. **Omega 3 Fatty Acids.** According to nutrition expert Susan Goodwin, "Omega 3 is good for you because it provides you a wide range of health benefits right from head to toe. They help promote normal body function, even promote good emotional health, weight loss and lower your chances of developing

cardiovascular problems such as heart disease and black arteries. There are also many research studies suggesting that these essential fatty acids help regulate brain function both in children and adults."[1] Some places to get Omega 3 fatty acids: flaxseed oil, salmon, sardines and walnuts.

5. **Black Beans.** According to an article at "Eat This!" black beans "are very high in fiber, folate, protein, and antioxidants, along with numerous other vitamins and minerals. Black beans make a complete protein when paired with brown rice, which is often why they are so commonly included in a vegetarian diet."[2]

A FEW OTHER THINGS I LIKE . . . THAT MIGHT SURPRISE YOU

1. **Coffee.** I have read a few studies lately that document the benefits of coffee! I was so happy to find those!!!

2. **Chocolate.** Dark chocolate not only tastes good . . . but it also has antioxidants in it!!

3. **Whole Grain Bread.** I really love bread . . . dipped in olive oil . . . or covered with peanut or almond butter . . . or toasted with jam. If the bread is whole grain, that means fiber . . . which is good!!

FIVE THINGS I AVOID

1. **Artificial Sweeteners.** No matter what color the packet, they are all bad for you. Seriously bad. Use honey, molasses, agave or Stevia instead.

2. **The White Stuff . . .** Stay away from white flour, white sugar and salt. There are so many healthier alternatives. For flour: lots of whole grain flours. For sweeteners: honey, molasses, agave, Stevia. For salt: natural sea salt or Himalayan salt (which still has some minerals left in it).

3. **Fast Food.** C'mon . . . you know you shouldn't be eating it!! Most fast foods are high in fat, stupid calories, carbohydrates, and too much artificial stuff!

4. **Processed Food.** If it's boxed, bagged, canned or jarred and has a list of ingredients on the label, it's processed. As scary as it seems, about 90 percent of the money that Americans spend on food is used to buy processed items.[3] Here are just a few reasons you might want to think twice before throwing that box of processed whatever into your shopping cart:

    - **Cancer:** Some synthetic chemicals used in the processed foods industry are known to have carcinogenic properties. In fact, a 7-year study, conducted by the University of Hawaii, of almost 200,000 people found that those who ate the most processed meats (hot dogs, bologna, and so on) had a 67 percent higher risk of pancreatic cancer than those who ate few or no processed meat products.

    - **Obesity:** Heavily processed foods are usually higher in sugar, fat and salt—and lower in nutrients and fiber—than the raw foods used to create them, leading to unhealthy weight gain and water retention. According to the World Health Organization, processed foods have contributed to the spike in obesity levels and chronic disease around the world.

    - **Heart Disease:** Many processed foods contain trans fatty acids (TFA), the dangerous type of fat that you don't want in your diet. TFAs give rise to LDL, the

dangerous cholesterol, and squash HDL, the good cholesterol.[4]

A recently conducted Harvard study found that women who avoid high-carb processed foods cut their heart disease risk by 30 percent.

5. **Bad Fats.** According to Kathleen M. Zelman, director of nutrition for WebMD, "We actually need fats—can't live without them, in fact. Fats are an important part of a healthy diet: They provide essential fatty acids, keep our skin soft, deliver fat-soluble vitamins, and are a great source of energizing fuel."[5]

   Dr. Zelman goes on to state that there are two groups of fats: saturated and unsaturated. Unsaturated fats are the "good fats" and include Omega-3s, which are found in fatty fish (salmon, trout, catfish, mackerel), and also flaxseed, walnuts, olives, avocados, hazelnuts, almonds, Brazil nuts, cashews, sesame seeds, pumpkin seeds, and olive, canola and peanut oils.

   Saturated fats and trans fats are the "bad fats." Saturated fats are found in animal products like meat, poultry skin, high-fat dairy and eggs. Trans fats are found in frying products, baked goods, cookies, icings, crackers, packaged snack foods, microwave popcorn and some margarine. You should try to avoid both saturated fats and, especially, trans fats.[6]

Okay . . . here is a sixth thing I avoid:

6. **Cigarettes.** This might seem obvious to some of you . . . and yet the number of young women who are smoking surprises me. While walking through an airport recently, I noticed a smoking room. There were so many young people in there. It just makes me sad.

   Smoking is not going to send you to hell . . . but you might get to heaven before you want to.

   Fifty years ago, we didn't know all the damage that smoking does, but now we do.

   It kills you.
   Really.
   And the death is a slow and painful one.
   It also ages you.

   Studies have been done, comparing twins—one who smoked and one who didn't. The skin of the one who smoked was far more wrinkled and leathery.[7]

   If you smoke, please stop. You have a destiny to fulfill . . . and we need you strong and healthy to do it!!

EIGHT REASONS TO MOVE YOUR TUSH!

The following information, based on studies from the Mayo Clinic, show why it is so important for you to get out there and move your tush! Exercising is a habit I wish I had started when I was in my twenties . . . so please get started now! You won't regret it . . . and you may even thank me later! ☻

1. **Exercise controls weight.** Exercise can help you avoid gaining excess weight and help you accomplish your weight loss goals. Physical activity burns calories—the more intense the activity, the more calories you burn. If you don't have time during your day to do an actual workout, you can get active throughout the day in simple ways—such as taking the stairs instead of the elevator or doing more household chores.

2. **Exercise combats health conditions and diseases.** Keeping active boosts your level of high-density lipoprotein (HDL, or "good" cholesterol) and decreases unhealthy triglycerides. This keeps your blood flowing smoothly and decreases your risk of cardiovascular diseases. Regular physical activity can even help you to prevent or manage a wide range of health problems, including stroke, metabolic syndrome, type 2 diabetes, depression, arthritis and certain types of cancer.

3. **Exercise improves mood.** Physical activity stimulates the production of various chemicals in your brain that may leave you feeling happier and more relaxed. You may also feel better about your appearance when you exercise regularly, which can boost your confidence and improve your self-esteem.

4. **Exercise boosts energy.** Regular physical activity improves muscle strength and increases endurance. When you perform physical activities, oxygen and nutrients are delivered to your tissues, which helps your cardiovascular system work more efficiently. This will give you more energy as you go about your daily life.

5. **Exercise promotes better sleep.** Regular physical activity can help you fall asleep faster and deepen your sleep. However, it is important not to exercise too close to bedtime, as that may make you too energized to fall asleep.

6. **Exercise puts the spark back into your sex life.** As mentioned under items 3 and 4 above, exercise can boost your energy and make you feel better about yourself, which may have a positive effect on your sex life. Regular physical activity can also lead to enhanced arousal for women, and men who exercise regularly are less likely to have problems with erectile dysfunction.

7. **Exercise can be fun.** Engaging in physical activity gives you time to unwind, enjoy the outdoors, or engage in activities that make you happy. Physical activity can also help you connect with family or friends in a fun social setting. Find a physical activity you enjoy, and just do it.[8]

8. **Exercise keeps your brain healthy!** Recent studies have found that aerobic exercise improves brain function among women who are at high risk for Alzheimer's and other forms of cognitive impairment.[9]

DEFLATING THE STRESS BALL

After my cancer diagnosis, I spent a few weeks in a hospital that offered a variety of treatments . . . both conventional and alternative.

One of the tests performed on me was a stress test.

As the doctor hooked me up to a machine, he asked, "Holly, how are you feeling? Do you feel like you are under stress?"

I responded, "Well, I know that I was diagnosed with cancer four months ago, but I think I am handling it well. I don't feel stressed."

He said, "Okay," and began the test.

When he was finished, he told me that in reality, my stress level was as if I were staring a roaring lion in the face. WOW! A roaring lion! That is some stress!! I had been totally unaware of it.

We all deal with stress—and, truthfully, not all stress is bad. Most of us would never get over negative behaviors or change or grow unless we experienced some stress.

Different things cause stress for each of us.

I have a fairly busy travel schedule. I go all around the globe, speaking at churches and conferences. I love that I get to do that. It is not stressful for me. But there are some people in my world who get very stressed by having to deal with packing and airports and the rush of travel. Some people also get stressed with change. Not me.

I tend to feel stress when relationships are under pressure. If I have to navigate a challenge in a friendship or in my marriage, I will feel a bit of stress.

Regardless of the cause, I needed to learn how to recognize when my body was under stress and how to relieve it.

TOP 10 STRESS RELIEVERS

The following information, also based on studies at the Mayo Clinic, give practical tips for handling the stresses that come your way. Incorporating these into your daily routine will give you the upper hand when stress threatens to take over.

1. **Get active.** (I know it seems as if I am harping on this!!) Being active is a great way to relieve stress. Anyone, regardless of their athletic ability or how long it's been since they got off the couch, can incorporate physical activity into their day. Whether you join a gym or just park your car farther across the parking lot from the store and walk, any physical activity can act as a stress reliever. Being physically active increases endorphins that lighten your mood and help you

rise above the irritations of the day. Any increase in activity helps—whether you take a walk, ride a bike, swim, tour a museum or put on some music and clean your house (LOL!). Do anything that increases your activity.

2. **Pray . . . quiet your soul.**
   When you pray, you want to focus your attention on the Lord and quiet the noise that may be crowding your mind and causing stress. Prayer allows you to find peace in God's presence and renew a sense of balance that benefits both your emotional well-being and your overall health.

3. **Laugh.** There is nothing like a good laugh!! You may need to begin with intentional efforts to look for humor in your day until you can see through the stress and laugh with genuine abandon. As you laugh, the weight of your mood can begin to lighten and your body will experience positive physical changes. Laughter will increases your heart rate and blood pressure, leaving you with a good, relaxed feeling. Seek out activities and people that will help you laugh—movies, YouTube clips, or an activity that you can share with a goofy friend.

4. **Connect.** Feeling stressed and irritable can make you feel anti-social. You probably don't want to share your bad mood with others or say things in the heat of the moment that you will regret, so you isolate yourself. Spend time with family and friends that can give you support, get you moving or focus your attention on something positive. Good relationships can keep you steady when your circumstances pull you in different directions. You can also find stress relief by serving others and feeling good about doing good. Meet a friend for coffee or a movie, reach out to a relative, serve those who are less fortunate, or get to church.

5. **Assert yourself.** Life is full of busyness—and great opportunities—but you can't do them all and maintain healthy balance in your life. It's okay to say no when your plate is full, or delegate some tasks. It may seem easier to do things yourself in the short run—to keep the peace, avoid conflict or get the job done right—but the long-term effect can be damaging to you and the needs of your family. Having your priorities out of synch can create stress, anger, bitterness and even the desire for revenge—the opposite of the peace you intended to create by doing it yourself.

6. **Sleep.** Stress can wreak havoc on your sleep patterns. All the noise in your life can dominate your thoughts, even when you try to rest and your sleep suffers. Your

body and mind need regular, quality time to sleep so they can recharge and be ready for the next day. Your sleep affects your mood, energy level, your ability to focus and your overall ability to function. Keeping a consistent bedtime routine that allows you time to unwind (music helps here), relax (eliminate distracting "noise") and get enough sleep will help calm trouble you have sleeping.

7. **Journal.** I am not a big journaler (not sure that is a word!), but I have heard from numerous people that putting their thoughts on paper helps them process stressful feelings. It doesn't matter what you write about, just put whatever is on your mind down on paper or on your computer. Sometimes just the process of getting it out helps relieve stress, other times, reflecting on what you write gives you perspective on what you are feeling and helps you address the stress you are experiencing.

8. **Get musical.** Music can be used in many ways to relieve stress. It can take your mind off the stress and help you relax, which lowers stress hormones in your body. It can also energize and entertain you if you turn up the volume and sing or dance along. Different personalities use music in different ways to improve their moods. The point is to help you focus your attention on something that you enjoy rather than all

the things you feel you should be doing that cause you stress. If music doesn't do this for you, any activity or hobby that helps you focus in this way will work—for some it will be gardening, drawing, or being creative by enjoying photography or jewelry making.

9. **Seek counsel.** It's OK to seek professional help when your personal efforts to handle stressors just aren't relieving your stress. This is especially true if stress is derailing your ability to handle daily tasks and responsibilities. If you feel overwhelmed or trapped, or if you worry excessively, a professional counselor or therapist can help you take positive steps in managing your stress.[10]

10. **Breathe.** According to Joseph E. Pizzorno, Jr. and Michael T. Murray in their book *Textbook of Natural Medicine*, deep breathing is a primary way to lower your body's stress responses. Deep breathing starts a cycle where your brain calms down and relaxes and in turn tells your body to do the same. Stress, that affects your body by increasing your heart rate, breathing and blood pressure, decreases as you breathe deeply and relax.[11]

WHAT DOES SLEEP DO FOR US?

Our understanding of the role of sleep in terms of our health has grown tremendously. We know that sleep has a huge impact on our ability to function both physically and mentally. We can't live without it! Studies in animals (rats, to be exact) have shown that sleep deprivation attacks the immune system and leads to death (the rats only lasted 3 to 5 weeks without REM and the other stages of sleep).

Sleep helps our nervous system stay healthy so that we can concentrate, have a strong memory, and perform well at physical and mental tasks. Extended sleep deprivation can result in serious mood swings and even hallucinations—not a good thing!

When we experience deep sleep, our bodies use that time to repair physical damage like what can result from stress and exposure to ultraviolet rays. So literally, deep sleep is "beauty sleep." Deep sleep also impacts our emotional health. The parts of our brains that work so hard during the day to manage our emotions, relationships and decision-making rest and rejuvenate during this time so that we can wake up and tackle the next day's emotional requirements—we need all the help we can get![12]

When we sleep, our bodies release growth hormones that help the growth and repair of damaged tissue. Getting generous amounts of deep sleep allows more growth hormones to be released into the body's bloodstream.[13]

Our bodies follow a 24-hour cycle. During this time, our bodies are on a schedule of automatically cleaning and rebuilding. Having healthy sleep patterns, helps our bodies perform these functions. For example, the liver goes through a cleansing process between 11:00 p.m. and 1:00 a.m. If you are awake during that time, your liver will not cleanse properly. Dr. Joseph Mercola has said that one hour of sleep before midnight is equal to four hours of sleep after midnight.[14]

Dr. Eve Van Cauter, a sleep researcher at the University of Chicago, said, "Americans sleep the least of [anyone in] modern countries. And they also . . . are the most overweight and obese. Perhaps it is worth thinking about the possibility that we don't sleep enough and therefore our appetites are disregulated."[15]

So . . . basically . . . most of us really do need eight hours of sleep a night in order to be firing on all cylinders!!!!!

A LITTLE RANDOM SLEEP NONSENSE . . .

Professor Chris Idzikowski, director of the U.K. Sleep Assessment and Advisory Service, analyzed six common sleeping positions—and found that each is linked to a particular personality type. Here's what your sleeping position says about you . . .

Fetus. Professor Idzikowski describes those who curl up in the fetus position as "tough on the outside but sensitive at heart." If this describes you, you may come off as a bit shy when you first meet someone, but as you become more comfortable you easily relax. This position is the most common—approximately 40 percent of the people studied preferred this position, and two-thirds of those people were women.

Log. Fifteen percent of the people studied prefer the "log" position. If you commonly find yourself lying on your side with both arms down by your side, you are a "log." You tend to be an easy-going, social person. You like being on the inside of any social situation and tend to be trusting of strangers. You also may have the tendency to be gullible.

Yearner. Thirteen percent of the people studied are "yearners." If you like to sleep on your side with your arms out in front of you, you are said to "have an open nature, but can be suspicious, cynical." As a yearner, your cautious nature can make you slow to make up your mind, and once you have, reluctant to change it.

Soldier. Eight percent of the people studied prefer the "soldier" position. If you usually find yourself lying on your back with both arms pinned to your sides, this is you. You are commonly a quiet and reserved person who doesn't like being in the limelight, but you feel it is important for people to live by high personal standards.

Freefall. Seven percent of the people studied are "free-fallers." If this is you, you prefer to lie on your stomach with your hands around your pillow, and your head turned to one side. As a freefaller you are a social person with a humorous bent that at the extreme can be a bit tactless. You can seem confident on the surface, but can be sensitive to criticism, and uncomfortable in extreme situations.

Starfish. Five percent of people are "starfish." If you prefer lying on your back with both arms up around your pillow, this is you. You are great at being a friend because you are generous with others, ready to listen and offer help when needed. You are more comfortable helping others rather than being the center of attention.[16]

TIPS FOR GETTING A GOOD NIGHT'S SLEEP

These tips are adapted from the article "How to Sleep Better" by Melinda Smith, Lawrence Robinson, Joanna Saisan and Robert Segal.

1. **Be consistent about the time you go to bed at night.**

2. **Boost melatonin production at night.** Melatonin helps you sleep and production is triggered by the absence of bright light. If you increase you exposure to light during the day and decrease it at night, you

will have an easier time falling asleep. During the day, get outside and light your workspace. At night, limit your screen time (TV, computers, backlit devices), use low lights when awake and keep your bedroom dark.

3. **Create an environment that invites sleep.** Most of us can't avoid all noise . . . after all, our neighbors have barking dogs!! ☻ But sound machines that produce white noise can be helpful. Temperature also matters—most people sleep better when the room temperature is about 65 degrees (Fahrenheit).

4. **Eat a light, early dinner.** Digesting is work and can keep you awake if you eat close to bedtime. What you eat makes a difference too. Save the spicy foods for lunch.

5. **Cut down on caffeine in the later afternoon.** We often underestimate the effect caffeine has on our sleep patterns—even 10 hours after consumption!

RELAXING BEDTIME RITUALS TO TRY

- Read a book or magazine by a soft light
- Take a warm bath

- Listen to soft music
- Do some easy stretches
- Wind down with a favorite hobby
- Listen to books on tape
- Make simple preparations for the next day[17]

H_2O . . . LIQUID GOLD!

Water, water, water!! There is no more important drink for us than water!

Water helps regulate body temperature.

It carries nutrients and oxygen to the cells.

It cushions joints.

It protects organs and tissues.

It removes toxins.

It maintains strength and endurance.

It makes up 92 percent of your blood plasma and 50 percent of everything else in your body.[18]

I have also heard that drinking water keeps our skin hydrated . . . so therefore reduces wrinkles!! Yippeeeee!!!

Dr. Don Colbert in his book *The Seven Pillars of Health* makes the following observations about drinking water:

> I saw singer Tina Turner in a television interview, and even though she was well into her sixties, her skin

> looked fabulous. She said it was because she drank at least two quarts of water every day. . . ; I believe that water is the single best beauty treatment on the planet. It keeps your skin supple, your eyes bright, and your body spry. Consider this: Remove water from plums, and you get prunes. Remove water from your skin, and you get wrinkles.[19]

Drink that water!!!

Most of us know that we are supposed to drink eight glasses a day . . . but do we do that???

Dr. F. Batmanghelidj writes, "Every twenty-four hours the body recycles the equivalent of forty thousand glasses of water to maintain its normal physiological functions." He adds, "If you think you are different and your body does not need [eight to ten glasses] of water [each day], you are making a major mistake."[20]

Purified water without chlorine is best. Since most tap water contains chlorine, it's a good idea to get a filter for your sink. They are not that expensive . . . and they're totally worth it.

I always carry a bottle of water with me and drink from it throughout the day.

Water is a resource often overlooked by those seeking to lose weight. Many times, dieters confuse hunger and thirst. They think they are hungry when actually they are dehydrated. Drinking water will not only hydrate the body, but also put a damper on those hunger pains coming from the pit of the stomach. Jordan Rubin, author of *The Great Physician's Rx for Health and Wellness,* suggests, "If you're trying to lose weight, drink an eight-ounce glass of water the next time you feel hungry. Drinking a glass a half hour before lunch or dinner will act like a governor on an engine, taking the edge off your hunger pangs and preventing you from raiding the fridge or pillaging the pantry."[21]

CATCH SOME RAYS!

I have a chest covered with brown spots (some call them sun spots) that are definitely NOT attractive. I wish I had listened to someone who gave me a little warning about sun baking! As a young woman, I slathered on baby oil and lay out in the hot midday sun for hours. That's what spring break was for! Not a good decision.

But staying totally out of the sun is not a good decision either. The sun, in moderation, is good for us!

Jordan Rubin writes, "While it's true that a small segment of the population experience higher rates of melanoma and other forms of skin cancer, I believe that's more because they lack adequate nutrients in their diets, especially antioxidant-rich fruits, vegetables, and healthy fats. Think about it: before the modern era, people used to spend much more time outside—and they didn't get skin cancer in the rates we see today."

Rubin concludes: "The reason we're having more skin cancer is not because we're getting too much sun. That can't be true because we're getting *far less* sun since so few people work outside these days. Getting sunlight is extremely important for our bodies because of the way the skin synthesizes vitamin D from the ultraviolet rays of sunlight. Exposure to the sun is a significant source of vitamin D."[22]

According to the National Institutes of Health, 10 to 15 minutes of sunlight are sufficient to allow vitamin D synthesis to occur. After that, it is wise to apply a natural sunscreen (SPF 15 or higher) to protect the skin.[23]

Vitamin D is a big deal. It actually isn't a vitamin, but a critical hormone that helps regulate the health of more than 30 different tissues and organs, including the brain. It is a super-powerful disease fighter that plays a role in regulating cell growth, the immune system and blood pressure.

So make sure you are getting a little sun . . . just not hours in the middle of the day! Because sunburn is not good! Neither are premature wrinkles and brown spots. Trust me . . . you won't like them!

HOW MUCH SHOULD YOU WEIGH?

We are very much aware that this is a sensitive subject. Some of you reading this may be underweight and dealing with an eating disorder. Please, please, please get some help!! You are so loved and valuable, and we need you strong. Some of you may be a few pounds overweight, and others of you may be obese.

Check out this website to get the answer to the question about how much you should weigh: www.howmuchshouldiweigh.org.

Remember, your body is not your own. It is the vessel that God entrusted to you to fulfill His purpose in you. You need to take care of it! Maybe you are just 10 pounds overweight. Well, if you keep gaining just 10 pounds every year, in 10 years you will be 100 pounds overweight . . . and losing 100 pounds is a lot harder than losing 10!

Most weight loss begins by changing our thinking.

Once you are on the journey to redirect your thoughts, there are many weight loss plans from which you can choose. Pick one, and just do it!

Twenty years from now, you don't want to be looking back and wishing you had done something sooner to improve your health. Decide today that you are going to do what's best for your one and only body.

You can do it!!

MORE, PLEASE!

(Additional reading)

The Great Physician's Rx for Health and Wellness by Jordan Rubin

The Seven Pillars of Health by Don Colbert, M.D.

Stress Less by Don Colbert, M.D.

None of These Diseases by S.I. McMillen, M.D. and David E. Stern, M.D.

4

What's in Your Wallet?

HOW TO MANAGE FINANCES

Too many people spend money they haven't earned, to buy things they don't want, to impress people they don't like.

WILL SMITH

MONEY MATTERS

Money means a lot of different things to a lot of people. Most of us have some and want more. We secretly dream of marrying a very rich (and handsome) man or winning the lottery, so we can finally afford the house with the pool . . . or at the very least, that designer purse we've been drooling over!

Some of us are taking active steps to create a strong financial future for ourselves. Some of us may even be reaping the benefits of years of budgeting and saving! Some of us really do enjoy crunching the numbers and finding new ways to invest in and increase our financial successes!

But for many of us, money is a rather stressful thing. We missed the "How to Balance Your Checkbook" elective in high school. Our parents may have fought a lot about finances, and their conflicts over the matter have left us with residual fears and anxiety when it comes to handling money. Some of us may have avoided the responsibility of managing our finances altogether, and that neglect has landed us in some rather sticky financial situations.

Jesus teaches us that how we view money—and what we do with ours—really does matter. In the Gospel of Luke, Jesus describes the attitude towards finances He wants to develop in us:

> Be generous. Give to the poor. Get yourselves a bank that can't go bankrupt, a bank in heaven far from bankrobbers, safe from embezzlers, a bank you can bank on. It's obvious, isn't it? The place where your treasure is, is the place you will most want to be, and end up being (Luke 12:33-34, THE MESSAGE).

Jesus in essence is saying that what we do with our money (our treasure) matters because it reveals the condition of our hearts . . . how we trust God, how we view ourselves, what we think about others . . .

Someone once told me that if you want to know what a person really values and cares about, you should take a look at his or her schedule and receipts.

We learn a lot about ourselves when we take a step back and examine our spending.

Are we fearful that God won't provide for us?

Do we struggle with a need to be instantly gratified, even if the cost is more than we can afford?

Do we invest in things that make us feel good about ourselves, but lack the ability to satisfy our souls in the long run?

Do we give generously, the way Jesus has given to us?

Or are we afraid that if we give, our own needs won't end up getting met?

When we make the commitment to honor God with our finances, we open our hearts to be transformed by the Holy Spirit! We begin to see where fear or doubt or insecurity or greed has been holding us back from the abundant and blessed life to which God has called us! When we begin to have Jesus' attitude in our hearts about finances, we become more like Him and discover new opportunities to be blessed by God to be a blessing in our world.

So this chapter is dedicated to you and me learning how to be smart with what's in our wallets . . . how to honor God with our finances . . . how to live generously . . . and how to manage wisely the resources with which God has blessed us.

For many of us, this may seem a bit scary—after all, it's the kind of stuff grown-ups do. You may be wondering if you are really ready for this type of responsibility . . .

You are! God wants to bless you and entrust you with finances that will make a huge difference in our world! He has all the wisdom you need to experience financial peace and prosperity. You can do this! Pull out your big-girl panties and get ready to grow into a money-savvy, generous and capable woman!

WHAT'S A TITHE, ANYWAY???

People have a lot of interesting ideas when it comes to what God thinks about money. Some people think that God hates money—that the poorer you are, the "holier" you are. Others think that God wants us to be rolling in the dough—that if you don't have a lot of money, you must not have enough faith. So which is it??? Does being a Christian mean being poor or being rich??? Does God even care about money???

The truth is, God does care about our finances . . .

He doesn't want to see us scraping by, always stressing about whether or not we can pay next month's rent. Neither does He want us greedily acquiring more and more "stuff" for our own selfish enjoyment.

God wants to provide for us financially both to meet our needs and to give us the resources to be a great financial BLESSING to others in our world. In short, God's will for you and me is that we should *be blessed to be a blessing*.

That kind of financial provision from God begins when we honor Him with our finances. When we manage our money in obedience to God's Word . . . when we discover what the Bible says to do with our money and choose to DO those things . . . we position ourselves to experience the incredible ways God can use our resources to make a huge difference in our own lives and the lives of those around us.

The very first way we honor God with our finances is by consistently tithing to our local church.

You may be wondering what in the world "tithing" is? Is that a fancy word for giving?

Tithing is the practice of *giving the first 10 percent of our income to the local church* as a biblical application of honoring God with our finances.

The word "tithe" literally means "10 percent." The Bible discusses tithing in depth in the book of Malachi:

> "Bring the whole *tithe* into the storehouse, that there may be food in my house. Test me in this," says the LORD Almighty, "and see if I will not throw open the floodgates of heaven and pour out so much blessing that you will not have room enough for it. I will prevent pests from devouring your crops, and the vines in your fields will not cast their fruit," says the LORD Almighty. "Then all the nations will call you blessed, for yours will be a delightful land," says the LORD Almighty (Mal. 3:10-12, emphasis added).

Jesus discussed giving multiple times, and His words challenge us to view our finances as a way of cultivating generosity towards our local churches and all those around us:

> Give away your life; you'll find life given back, but not merely given back—given back with bonus and blessing. Giving, not getting, is the way. Generosity begets generosity (Luke 6:38, THE MESSAGE).

The Early Church took Jesus' words to heart and gave even more than 10 percent of their income to meet the needs of others:

> They devoted themselves to the apostles' teaching and to the fellowship, to the breaking of bread and to prayer. Everyone was filled with awe, and many wonders and miraculous signs were done by the apostles. All the believers were together and had everything in common. Selling their possessions and goods, they gave to anyone [who] had need. Every day they continued to meet together in the temple courts. They broke bread in their homes and ate together with glad and sincere hearts, praising God and enjoying the favor of all the people. And the Lord added to their number daily those who were being saved (Acts 2:42-47).

Tithing is the first step in honoring God with our finances. When we actively tithe to our local churches, we develop a growing trust in God's provision. We begin to see God's blessings in new ways, not only in our finances, but also in every other area of our lives!

We also develop a heart of generosity! We begin to understand that it really is better to give than to receive. We become a part of seeing lives eternally changed by the message of Jesus as we actively tithe to our local churches. As we help finance

God's plans in people's lives, we ourselves are transformed. Our hearts enlarge towards God's plans and people's lives . . .

In short, we become more like Jesus as we tithe.

If you haven't yet made the decision to tithe to your local church, don't put it off! Begin tithing today! You may need to reallocate some of your spending budget. Maybe you will have to cut back on your shoe shopping or eat out fewer times a week. Maybe tithing seems like a big stretch of faith for you right now.

Whatever your financial situation may be, you can confidently trust God! His way is the best way! He is your perfect heavenly Father who loves you as His very own daughter. You are precious to Him. He won't withhold from you anything that you need. As you step out in faith and choose to honor and obey God with your finances, God will take care of you every step of the way! He will provide in every situation exactly what you need! He loves you, and His desire is to bless you!

> If God gives such attention to the appearance of wildflowers—most of which are never even seen—don't you think he'll attend to you, take pride in you, do his best for you? What I'm trying to do here is to get you to relax, to not be so preoccupied with *getting*, so you can respond to God's *giving*. People who don't know God and the way he works fuss over these things, but you know both God and how he works. Steep your life in God-reality, God-initiative, God-provisions. Don't worry about missing out. You'll find all your everyday human concerns will be met (Matt. 6:30-33, THE MESSAGE).

JUST SAY NO TO PLASTIC

I (Nicole) remember the first letter I ever received from Visa. I was 18 years old, and the president of Visa was "personally" writing me to congratulate me on my pre-approval! According to Mr. President, I had a $1,500 credit line waiting to be used! All I had to do was call the 1-800 number to activate my very own credit card.

Wow! Me?! I was surprised to find out that the big shots over at the bank were interested in giving li'l ol' me my very own credit card! I wasn't even out of high school yet, and I was already approved for my own plastic! And $1,500?! (When you're 18 years old and about to go to college, $1,500 sounds like a lot of money!)

Needless to say, I called the bank and talked to a very friendly representative—who assured me that having a credit card was a part of being a grown-up, and that all the cool kids were doing it . . . Okay, maybe he didn't say that, but he did convince me that having a credit card was crucial to living on my own. In his words, it was an "essential step" towards being a financially stable individual in today's world, and without it I would never be able to "establish good credit" for future purchases and investments.

That phone call cost me thousands of dollars over the next few years! The credit card that I told myself would only be used for emergencies became very helpful for the

"Starbucks-run-emergency" and the "I-have-nothing-to-wear-emergency" and the "who-needs-a-budget-anyway-emergency" and . . . well, you get the idea.

All the while, every time I swiped my card at the store, interest charges were stacking up a mile high against me!

Proverbs teaches us that "the rich rules over the poor, and the borrower becomes the lender's slave" (Prov. 22:7, NASB).

I certainly felt like a slave to my credit card bill! Any extra money I earned each month went straight to the credit card company . . . but even so, the total payoff amount never seemed to go down! My debt was hindering my ability to create a real savings account for myself, and I was limited in terms of how I could financially plan and dream for my future!

I wasn't alone.

There are more than 1.3 billion credit cards in circulation in America.

American consumer debt totals more than $2.7 trillion.

Forty-five percent of American credit card holders make only the minimum payments on their consumer debt.

The average balance per credit card-holding household is more than $9,300.[1]

Yikes! I knew I needed some help, stat! If I didn't come up with a game plan, I was never going to get out of debt.

I started to read books on finances. I mapped out a strict budget that would allow more money to go towards paying off my credit card balance. I asked my friends to hold me accountable to that not-so-friendly-to-a-girl's-new-wardrobe budget!

Then the big moment came. I got my big-girl scissors out and made a very big-girl decision to cut that stupid piece of plastic into tiny little bits. It was scary to see my financial security blanket chopped up and lying in pieces at the top of the trash. But it was also liberating.

I paid off my credit card bill later that year. Over the next year and a half, I went on to pay off my student loans and began living debt free!

I am now able to plan for my future in ways I never thought possible. I can give more financially to my church and to nonprofits than ever before! I am able to live generously towards my friends without hesitation!

This kind of financial freedom begins when we say no to the crazy cycle of accumulating more and more debt. Your ability to reach your dollar-sign goals AND live a generous life to the full begins when you pull out the scissors and JUST SAY NO TO PLASTIC!

STEPS TOWARD SAYING GOODBYE TO DEBT!

These steps come from concepts presented in *Dave Ramsey's Financial Peace University*, which is a great program for anyone serious about achieving financial success!

1. **Quit borrowing!** Avoid the temptation to take out a loan to pay off a credit card, or to use a credit card to make your car payment. Cut up those credit cards and repeat after me, "Plastic is not my friend." Now say it again . . . only this time stop trying to figure out how you can tape the card back together for a quick trip to the mall. "Plastic is not my friend." Very good.

2. **Save, save, save!** Be willing to make BIG adjustments to your spending plan. You might have to say no to trips to the mall, eating out, and even your favorite Starbucks Frappucino for a while. In order to rid yourself of debt, you need to make the tough sacrifices now. Remember: No pain, no gain.

3. **Prayer works!** God's desire is to see you debt-free! When you commit to a plan of tithing, budgeting, saving, and paying off debt, you can trust God to bless your hard work in some MIRACULOUS ways. God blesses plans that bless Him!

4. **Sell what you can**. Do you really need that brand new car with the expensive payments? Do you have to have a timeshare in Cancun? Is the furniture in the guest room really essential? Why are those seven bridesmaid's dresses still hanging in the corner of your closet? Be willing to downsize and eliminate items that could help provide for your financial freedom!

5. **Work it!** Pick up an extra shift at your job. Babysit one night a week. Work part-time as a barista. Use

the extra income to pay off your debt. This may be a humbling thing to do, depending on what season of life you are in, but God helps the humble! A little humility is a small price to pay compared to the investment you'll be making towards a stronger financial future!

6. **Apply the "debt snowball."** In Dave Ramsey's words, "The idea of the snowball is simple: pay minimum payments on all of your debts except for the smallest one. Then, attack that one with intensity! Every extra dollar you can get your hands on should be thrown at that smallest debt until it is gone. Then, you attack the second one. Every time you pay a debt off, you add its old minimum payment to your next debt payments. So, as the snowball rolls over, it picks up more snow."[2]

THE BIG B-WORD!

No, no. Not that word. The other B-word . . . BUDGET.

Most of us have love-hate relationships with our budgets. We love that sticking to a monthly budget means we are actively taking steps towards our financial goals. But sticking to that monthly budget also means we may have to say no to those cute boots we saw at Nordstrom! So unfair!

However we feel about the idea of a monthly budget, we have to acknowledge how very essential it is to our financial well-being!

There's no way around it . . . If we want to live financially successful lives, we have to develop *love-love* relationships with our monthly budgets! The monthly budget creates an actual plan for financial success. It acts as the bridge from where we are now to where we want to be in our financial futures!

So take some time this week to sit down with your bank account statement and a list of your monthly expenses, bills and income. Create a plan that you can live by . . . and pray that as you commit to a monthly budget, God will bless you financially! Ask God to show you how to become more responsible with your money . . . because at the end of the day, it all belongs to Him anyway! When we learn to be great stewards of our finances, we become the daughters to whom our heavenly Father can entrust even more!

SAVINGS: THE BIG-GIRL PIGGY BANK

Most of us have been told at some point—probably by our mothers—that we should "always be prepared for a rainy day." We have to admit, living in Southern California means we don't have to be prepared for rain very often. (In fact, only a few days a year. Okay, now we're just bragging about the gorgeous sunny weather we live in.)

Of course, our moms weren't really talking about the weather. They wanted us to be prepared for the challenges (as well as the opportunities) that life would throw at us.

Our finances are one area where preparation is crucial. Over the course of our lives, we will face many unexpected financial costs and opportunities. We should plan NOW to be prepared for these events in the future.

There's the last-minute flight home . . . or the check-engine light that goes on in the car . . . or the visit to the emergency room . . . or the cutbacks at work. Then there's the exciting new business opportunity . . . or the fundraiser we want to contribute to . . . or the kitchen remodeling we've been dreaming about since we first moved into the house.

These are the things in life we need to be financially prepared for . . . and it all begins with establishing a savings plan!

HERE ARE SOME QUICK TIPS AND SIMPLE WAYS TO SAVE

1. **Open your very own savings account with your bank, if you haven't already.** It's so easy that you can do it online or over the phone with most major banks!

2. **Do whatever you can to get $1,000 dollars into your savings account immediately!** Tighten your budget or pick up extra hours at work. This first $1,000 becomes your "emergency fund" for those unexpected events that life throws your way!

3. **Get out of debt ASAP!** Once you have your $1,000 "emergency fund" in the bank, shift your focus to becoming debt-free. The sooner you are out of debt, the faster you can start taking the money you've

been spending to pay off bills and investing it in your savings!

4. **Set a goal of having two to six months' worth of income in savings!** This may take some time, but it will provide you with a new sense of financial security as you navigate different seasons of life!

5. **Each month, try to put at least 10 percent of your income into savings.** The basic rule of thumb is to tithe 10 percent of your income, save 10 percent of your income, and live off the remaining 80 percent of your income (including giving generously as you are able).

FINDING THE DRESS FOR LESS AND OTHER SHOPPING TIPS

Who says you have to break the bank to look cute or enjoy a fun night out with your girlfriends? Below are some easy tips for getting the most bang for your buck!

1. Stop by your local mechanic's shop once a month to get the air pressure in your tires adjusted for free. Fifteen minutes a month can save you hundreds of dollars in new tires down the road!

2. Instead of hitting up the mall, try a consignment shop or second-hand store! You can find some really funky vintage pieces or the perfect pair of gently worn jeans to add to your wardrobe without having to empty your wallet!

3. Did you know that your local library has DVDs you can borrow for free? Enjoy a girls' night in with a classic romantic comedy, courtesy of your public library card!

4. Unplug those appliances that aren't in use. Most people spend much more than they need to on their electric bills, simply because they forget to unplug the hairdryer, coffeemaker, laptop and iPhone charger!

5. See if your favorite restaurant has a "happy hour" and score a great deal on a yummy meal! Even if they don't, you can always split a large entrée with a friend!

6. Say hello to the great outdoors! Instead of spending $25 at the movie theatre, opt for spending the day outside . . . Enjoy a hike, a day at the beach, or a picnic in the park with friends!

7. Clip those coupons! You can also find great deals online through websites like www.Groupon.com to help you save money on your everyday spending!

8. Discuss a simpler style with your hairstylist. Find a cut and color that require less frequent salon visits and fewer dollar signs!

EIGHT TIPS FOR THE WORKING GIRL

It's easy for us to get comfortable in familiar circumstances. If we're not careful, jobs we once were ecstatic about become, over time, jobs that simply pay the bills. We once woke up early, excited to go to work. Now we crawl out of bed after hitting the snooze button three times and wishing we had more caffeine to get us through the day! We once gladly put in extra hours; now we add extra minutes to our lunch breaks!

In short, we get bored.

Or worse, we develop a sense of entitlement. We assume that we will get a promotion or a raise. We expect the corner office or the successful business or the fat paycheck without remembering that all those rewards (and the responsibilities that come with them) require hard work and dedication—or as the Bible puts it . . . FAITHFULNESS.

It doesn't matter if you are a Starbucks barista or an unpaid intern or a substitute teacher or a marketing consultant or a pastor. We have each been given different opportunities and interests. God has placed a specific job in each of our hands . . . but what He has given us matters less than what we choose to do with it. God grants more opportunity to those who prove themselves faithful with what is *currently* in their hands, regardless of how little or big it may seem to others. God can confidently give more to those who understand that they have been entrusted (not entitled), and who do their best to be faithful stewards of what they have been given!

Below are some tips for making the most of the current job God has placed in your hands. Whether or not it is your "dream job," it is a chance for you to grow and to develop the character and skills you may need later on. Perhaps God is using your *present* job to prepare you for the *future* opportunities you dream about!

1. **Early is the new on-time.** Make sure to arrive early to your shift at work or to your meetings. No one likes to hear the "traffic was so bad" or "I overslept" excuses!

2. **Be proactive.** If you feel like you have a job that isn't challenging you, then make it your responsibility to challenge yourself! My (Nicole's) dad is the hardest-working man I have ever met! As a manager, he always taught me that I should never just stand around waiting for someone to give me work to do. He told me that the best employees are the ones who have eyes to see a problem . . . and then proactively fix it! Great employees seek out ways to do *more* for their companies or organizations.

3. **Create solutions, not problems, for your boss.** Be the most uncomplicated employee you can be. By uncomplicated, we mean someone who doesn't take

things personally, isn't easily offended, and consistently has a great attitude! If your supervisor asks you to solve a problem, do everything you can to come up with a solution using the resources available to you. Be the kind of employee that makes your boss's job easier, not harder!

4. **Stay away from water cooler gossip.** Avoid workplace drama. Don't participate in gossip, and keep confidential information confidential! Make sure that you speak highly of your boss and your coworkers when they aren't around.

5. **Be a team player!** Work well with those around you. Be someone who adds to the productivity of the team and cares for the needs of teammates. Don't vie for recognition; instead, find opportunities to help coworkers shine. Don't fight for the spotlight, but rather trust that God will promote you and give you favor at the right time. *He will never ask you to sabotage someone else's success to get to the top.*

6. **Learn to communicate well with different personalities.** Not everyone you work with thinks or communicates like you. That's a good thing! The world would be very boring if everyone thought and spoke the same exact way! But truth be told, these enlivening

differences can also make for some misunderstandings in the workplace. Go out of your way to get to know the people you work with, and make every effort to communicate respect and care to each and every one of them. Read books and listen to presentations that can help you improve your communication skills in the workplace.

7. **Integrity matters.** Don't allow "little white lies" to undermine your potential. Refuse the temptation to cut corners on the expense report, take a few dollars for yourself out of the cash register, call in sick so you can enjoy a "free" day off from work, leave the office a few minutes early without telling anyone, or take credit for something you didn't do. The work you do isn't just for your company or your boss—it's for Jesus . . . and the best way we can honor Jesus at work is in the details, whether or not people notice!

8. **Represent Jesus!** The people you work with have front-row seats to the way you do life. Pray and look for opportunities to talk about Jesus in ways that are welcomed and encouraging. While remembering that no one is perfect, commit to being the best example of a Jesus-follower you can be at your job! Who knows . . . you may be the only representation of Jesus your coworkers will ever see . . . and the one who will lead them to their own authentic relationships with Him!

TEN WAYS TO BE GENEROUS

1. **Treat a friend to lunch.** Bonus points if you are able to pay for the check without them noticing!

2. **Pay for the order of the person behind you at Starbucks.** I love doing this! People are always surprised that a complete stranger would practice random generosity!

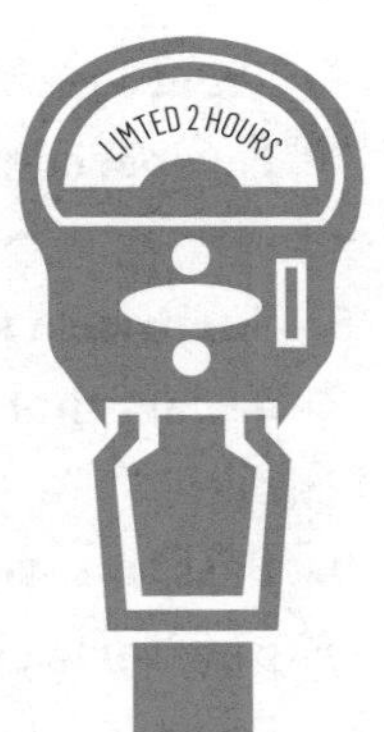

3. **Add quarters to someone's parking meter.** Save someone from one more parking ticket!

4. **Sponsor a child.** Help a child in a developing nation receive food, medical attention and education simply by making a monthly donation. When children are given opportunities for transformed lives, they will ultimately transform their communities. For more information, visit www.compassion.com.

5. **Give above and beyond your regular tithe to your local church.** Set a goal to give more in one year than you ever have before, and know that your generosity will make an eternal impact in the life of someone else!

6. **Surprise a family member or friend who is struggling to make ends meet with a gift card to a grocery store or nearby gas station.** Your generosity may be an answer to their prayers!

7. **Treat a girlfriend to a mani-pedi.** No special occasion . . . just because!

8. **Surprise a friend with a piece of costume jewelry or a scarf that totally reminds you of her!**

9. **Pass on your maternity clothes or your baby's newborn clothes to a woman in your world who just found out she's having a baby!**

10. **Buy lunch for a homeless person.** Make sure to let them know that you are praying for them, and that you care! Don't be stingy; treat them to whatever meal they want!

MORE, PLEASE!

(Additional reading)

The Total Money Makeover by Dave Ramsey

Managing God's Money by Randy Alcorn

Rich Dad Poor Dad by Robert T. Kiyosaki

The Blessed Life by Robert Morris

Suze Orman's Financial Guidebook by Suze Orman

5

Doing Life Together

HOW TO NAVIGATE FRIENDSHIPS

A friend is a present you give yourself.

ROBERT LOUIS STEVENSON

WE'RE ALL IN THIS TOGETHER

I have to admit, I've never really understood the *High School Musical* phenomenon. I remember high school . . . and it certainly did not include breaking out into spontaneous song with the star athlete and cheerleader in the school cafeteria.

But I will give props to one song from the film. It's called "We're All in This Together." Here's why I like it: because it's true.

We are all in this together. Being human is not an individual, isolated experience. It's corporate. It's social. It's communal.

God puts it this way at the very beginning of the Bible: "It is not good for the man to be alone" (Gen. 2:18).

The great South African civil rights activist and Christian leader, Desmond Tutu, has written and delivered numerous speeches on this very subject. In his words, "We can be human only together."

Christian author and pastor, Eugene Peterson, who paraphrased and created *THE MESSAGE* version of the Bible, wrote, "We need community to complete our humanity."[1]

You and I were made to flourish and find fulfillment in healthy, genuine relationships. Without them, we will never experience the fullness of God's love for us and will never have the support we need to live out His extraordinary plans for our lives.

We weren't created to solve all of life's problems on our own. We need each other! We really are all in this together!

We need one another's wisdom and experiences. We need mentors who encourage us to become more like Jesus and enjoy the abundant life He has for us. We need friends to cheer us on when we face the larger-than-life challenges that come our way.

Life truly can become a grand, beautiful adventure when we have healthy friendships. This chapter is all about giving you the tools you need to find, grow and strengthen great friendships . . . the kind of friendships that bring levels of joy to your heart you didn't know were possible!

WHERE MY FRIENDS AT?!

We have talked to many women who faced crises, whether financial or health-related or marital, and felt all alone; or worse, they expressed that they got into the situations they were in partly because of the influence of poor friendships in their lives.

In conversation, they usually reveal how hard it has been for them to find quality friends they could rely on and trust.

Maybe you feel the same way. Maybe you have been betrayed by a friend in the past and now find it hard to trust. Maybe you just moved to a new city or started at a new school and are having a hard time meeting people. Maybe you never put much thought into choosing friends and have just sort of defaulted to having close friendships with the people you happen to spend the most time with.

We need to ask you a few questions.

Do you want great, life-giving, exciting friendships?

Do you want friendships that encourage, inspire and challenge you?

Do you want friendships that help you wholeheartedly follow Jesus and pursue His plans for your life?

Do you want friendships that endure and are able to overcome the many storms life will bring?

If you do, the good news is that God wants the very same things for YOU! He created you for relationships—a thriving, loving relationship with Jesus and thriving, loving relationships with other people! He wants you to experience the wonder and happiness found in genuine, healthy friendships!

The first step toward developing quality friendships is deciding to *be the type of friend you are looking for.*

We can only expect from others what we are willing to give. In many areas of life, we tend to attract the qualities that we ourselves are exuding.

What qualities do you wish for in your close friends? A good sense of humor, an adventurous spirit, a good listener, a passion for Jesus . . . ?

Take a few minutes to come up with your own list of qualities. Then reflect and pray about which of these traits you currently have, and where you can grow and become a better friend to those around you . . .

TEN QUALITIES OF A GREAT FRIEND

1. She knows how to laugh and have a good time!
2. She listens well.
3. She doesn't hold grudges.
4. She is kind to others.
5. She is generous.
6. She refrains from silly gossip.

7. She is confident in her own skin.

8. She always tells the truth.

9. She has an authentic and growing relationship with Jesus Christ.

10. She dreams big and pursues God's purposes for her life!

STEP OUT OF YOUR COMFORT ZONE

One of the best things about being part of our local church is the diversity of friendships it has brought us. We both have friends of all ages, backgrounds, shapes and sizes . . . and our lives are better for it! Each friend adds a new, vibrant hue that colors our life experience! Our world gets brighter and larger every time we step out of our comfort zones and invest in friendships with people who are different than we are! (It's also a great preview of what heaven will be like!) Here are some types of friendships to pray for and pursue in your life:

1. **Friends with DIFFERENT personalities.** Are you the type that would rather talk with one person for 45 minutes at a party than chat it up with everyone in the room? Chances are you will have an opportunity to develop a friendship with someone who is the

life of the party. It's like she always carries confetti in her purse!

It's easy to feel more comfortable with people who think like we do, but if we only connect with people who have similar personalities, then we will be missing out on friendships that draw the very best out of us. Plus, life quickly becomes boring when we surround ourselves with people just like us!

2. **Friends of a DIFFERENT age.** We can gain a great deal of wisdom by hanging around an older woman who has a genuine faith in Jesus. She has weathered a few storms, and we need to hear how she did it! Are you married? Spend some time with someone who has been married for more than a minute . . . and still likes her husband! Are you trying to start a business? Learn from a woman who has successfully built her business from scratch. Make sure to connect with women who can encourage and help you as you navigate different seasons of life.

Now, remember what we talked about back at the beginning of this book? No matter what your age is, you are an OLDER woman. You may still be trying to wrap your mind around this idea, but it doesn't need to be depressing. ☻ Right now, someone who is a few years younger than you are could use your advice and support. Have you graduated from college? I guarantee there is a younger woman who is pulling out her hair trying to study for exams. She needs YOU. Have you successfully paid off your student loans without signing away your firstborn? There's a younger woman who is in debt up to her eyeballs. She needs YOU. There's a young woman who just got her heart broken and doesn't know how she can ever love again. Perhaps you've kissed a few frogs before marrying your prince. That heart-broken woman needs YOU. Make sure to reach out and encourage the younger women in your world. You can be the friend you wish you had when you were her age.

3. **Friends from a DIFFERENT culture.** We have Latino friends. We have Asian friends. We have African-American friends. We have Caucasian friends. We have multiracial friends. Our friendship world is a melting pot, and we love it! Because of our friends, each of us has been exposed to more cultures, traditions and ways of doing life than we ever thought possible!

The apostle Paul wrote, "In Christ's family there can be no division into Jew and non-Jew, slave and free, male and female. Among us you are all equal. That is, we are all in a common relationship with Jesus Christ" (Gal. 3:28, THE MESSAGE). Jesus never intended for us to remain segregated. Through faith in Jesus, we discover what it means to live in racial harmony with one another. If we are ever going to bring lasting change to our world, that racial harmony must be more than a poetic, romanticized ideal. It has to affect how we do life in a personal way. We must be honest about our prejudices and hurts . . . and choose to overcome them with reconciliation and grace. When we embrace friends with different last names, languages, skin tones and traditions, we show the world that through Jesus it is possible to love one another!

4. **Friends with DIFFERENT interests.** Are you Ms. Athlete of the Year? Is your idea of a good time rock climbing or an intense game of flag football? Or is your idea of a pleasant afternoon a mani-pedi followed by a shopping spree with the girls?

   Whatever your interests are, make sure to build friendships with people whose interests are *different*. I (Nicole) love indie rock and alternative music . . . and I (Holly) love the sound of new country! A good friend of ours loves classical music and operas. We've had some great and hilarious conversations about music! She's even schooled us on what different operas are about. (She explains them like they're movie plots, and throws in a couple of explosions to keep our attention.) We now know a thing or two about operas! Who knew?

Our world becomes larger when we open ourselves to the differing interests our friends have! Every now and again, we even become smarter because of them! ☻

FRIENDSHIP CIRCLES

Not everyone you meet will end up being your BFF. Some will be people you routinely see at church or in your apartment complex—people you stop and say hi to when you run into them. Others will become friends you hang out with more regularly. A few will become the kind of friend you call when you just broke up with your boyfriend or he popped the question or your baby just said his first word. These are the friends who know more about us than anyone else does . . . and who love and respect us more than anyone else does.

But how do we know who falls into what category of friendship? How do we figure out who should stay acquaintances and who should gain entrance into the deeper levels of our trust and confidence? Below are three different friendship zones, with brief descriptions of qualities friends in each zone should display. Think about your current friendships and make sure you are placing people in the right friendship zones. There may be some friends who need to be relocated to another zone . . .

Zone 1:
Your Closest Friends
- Display a genuine love for Jesus
- Inspire and challenge you in your faith
- Give you biblical advice
- Hold you accountable when needed
- Have earned trust over time
- Celebrate and support you
- Have integrity in decision-making
- Have fun doing life with you!
- Are a real friend to your future!

Zone 2:
Friends To Hang With
- Have similar values as you
- Demonstrate qualities that are trustworthy
- Make responsible decisions
- Easy to get along with
- Are considerate of others

Zone 3:
Acquaintances
- Spend time with you every now and again
- Fun to be around
- Have similar interests

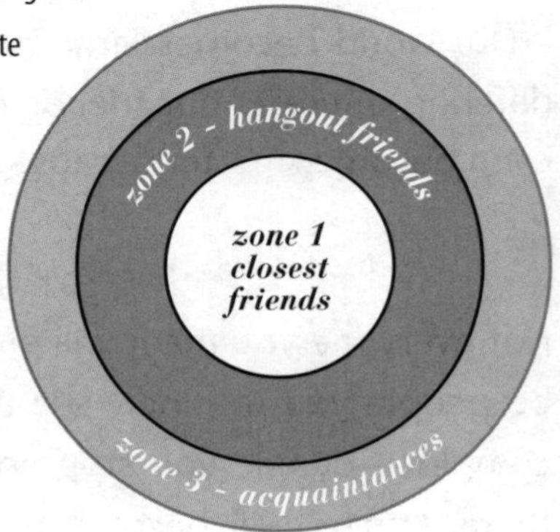

WARNING SIGNS OF TOXIC FRIENDSHIPS

1. **She is possessive.** In healthy friendships, the other person isn't jealous of other friendships you have. In fact, a friend should encourage you to broaden your friendship circle!

2. **She makes no effort.** It's disappointing, but sometimes we want a friendship more than the other person does. If you are always there for her, but she's never around for you, there's a problem. The effort made in friendships should be reciprocal; both parties should invest the time and energy to care for one another.

3. **She doesn't share many of your values.** Our values shape our actions, which ultimately shape our lives. If two friends don't share similar values, then inevitably their lives will head in different directions. It's important to have friends who are different from us, but when it comes to our closest friendships, we need to have mutual values. Make sure your closest friendships are with women who have a genuine faith in Jesus and are pursuing His plans for their lives.

4. **She compares herself to you.** Stay clear of the comparison game . . . because no one ever wins! Avoid comparing your weight, your salaries, your opportunities, or your talents and abilities. Comparisons only breed insecurities and jealousy.

5. **She can't keep her mouth shut.** If you are friends with someone who is always gossiping to you about other friends, you can be sure she is gossiping about YOU when you aren't around. People who are careless with their words are not people you can trust. Be around

people who speak highly of others and who refrain from contributing to or listening to hurtful gossip.

6. **She holds grudges.** No one's perfect. We all make mistakes. We say the wrong thing or forget a birthday. Make sure your friends are people who can address hurts quickly and forgive. No one likes to be continually reminded of something they did years ago or feel like there is a record being held against them by those they love. Cultivate friendships where people are mature in handling conflict and moving past hurts and miscommunications.

7. **She never lets you know what's really going on.** Emotionally mature friendships consist of two people who can honestly and respectfully share their feelings. Over time, they let their guards down and allow each other to know when they are going through difficult times. When someone is overly guarded, she excludes you from opportunities to be a genuine friend to her.

8. **She lacks character.** A friend who lies to avoid consequences or steals from the cash register or consistently flakes on your plans is NOT a good friend. You may care about this person, but you can't save her or fix her by being a better friend. They only way someone can change her character is by making the choice to

do so herself. We experience a lot of heartbreak and disappointment when we try to change people or expect them to give what they are unwilling or unable to give.

9. **She is inconsiderate.** Good friends appreciate and affirm each other. They value each other's efforts and the time given to the friendship. When someone doesn't communicate gratitude, she diminishes the other person's value as a friend. A friendship that consists of one friend always demanding or expecting another person to do something for her is just plain TOXIC.

10. **The friendship is boring.** The longer we know someone, the easier it is to fall into a rut. We eat at the same restaurant and order the same meal. We talk about the same things. We go to the same movie theatre and see the same type of romantic comedy. Traditions are comforting, but make sure to create new and fresh experiences with your friends. Take up a new hobby together. Visit a museum. Plan an adventure together.

FRIENDSHIP BOOSTERS

1. **Saying "thank you."** Maintain a level of gratitude toward your friend. Saying a simple "thank you" when she buys you a coffee or offers to pick up your kids from school goes a long way. Drop your friend a note or send her a thank you card sharing just how grateful you are for her friendship!

   Communicate that you don't take the friendship for granted and that you truly appreciate your friend!

2. **Celebrate each other!** Each of your friends is uniquely wired with a different personality, traits, background and interests. Celebrate your differences while focusing on your similar values! Don't secretly wish your friend were more like you. Maybe your friend is a detail-minded organizer, and you are a fly-by-the-seat-of-your-pants free spirit. Don't let that frustrate you. Be happy you have a friend who can bring a little organization to your fun spontaneity!

   No one likes to feel merely tolerated in a friendship. Your friends want to be celebrated! Applaud their uniqueness and learn to complement one another's strengths and weaknesses.

3. **Cheer each other on!** Is your friend studying hard for an exam? Did she just get engaged? Is she trying to overcome a bad habit or lose a few pounds? Is she working hard at getting out of debt?

Be her biggest cheerleader! Assure her that she's got what it takes and that you are there to support her however you can. Be willing to go out of your way to show that you care and that you've got her back! That may mean you hit up the gym again or find things to do together other than perusing the mall.

I (Nicole) remember when Holly was diagnosed with breast cancer a few years ago. The diagnosis began a dramatic journey on which she learned more about how to eat right and avoid toxic behaviors that jeopardize good health. She said goodbye to processed foods filled with sugar and chemicals, and she embraced a healthier, organic diet. She changed her soap, lotions, shampoos, and even her deodorant to natural products. She invested in water purifiers and began taking more raw vitamins and shots of wheatgrass than I knew were humanly possible to consume!

Even though I loved my donuts and soda and lard-infested refried beans and oh-so-yummy bacon . . . I loved my good friend and mentor even more. I couldn't do everything for her; in fact, there was a lot I couldn't do for her that I wish I could (for one, zap the cancer away!). But, one thing I knew I could do was walk alongside her on her health journey. So I, along with a few other friends, also gave up the unhealthy and ridiculously tasty foods for salads and wheatgrass and raw almonds.

Holly has been cancer-free for a few years now! Woohoo! Praise Jesus! In addition, both of us have discovered a much healthier way of taking care of the bodies God gave us!

You never know where being a friend's biggest fan will take you. It might mean changing habits or letting go of what's comfortable, but I guarantee it's an adventure worth taking!

4. **Laugh a lot.** There's nothing quite as sweet to the soul as a good laugh with a friend! One of my (Holly's) best friends started to become my friend because one day we found ourselves laughing at the same situation. Another friend of ours had a very public mishap with a glass door that still makes us laugh so hard that tears stream down our faces if we just think about it! And still another friend makes up the most ridiculous songs about random everyday events just to make us laugh! With some friends, we share inside jokes that have been going on for years! Make sure not only to

talk about the serious stuff, but also to have fun with your friends. Everyone needs girlfriends they can let their hair down in front of and just be girls with!

5. **Listen.** You never stop learning about people if you listen hard enough. Make sure to make time to be the person your friend can talk to when she needs someone to listen to her. When you really actively listen, you discover how to pray for and offer support to your friend. You also learn about her hopes, dreams, passions and fears. If you listen long enough, you will find out things you never knew, like:
   "I went skydiving once."
   "I backpacked through Europe."
   "I was adopted."
   "I studied to be an engineer before changing majors."
   "I've always been a bit fearful in this area."
   "I was abused as a child."
   Listening unites hearts more than talking does. Maybe your friend does not need to hear your opinion right now. Maybe she just needs you to listen.

FRIENDSHIP KILLERS

1. **Being too busy.** We lead very busy lives, and sometimes, in our busyness, we sacrifice quality time spent with

friends. If we aren't careful, our friendships can get put on the back burner. Friendships are crucial to our happiness and success in life! As your life gets fuller, make sure to continue to invest in quality friendships, even if that means grabbing coffee at the airport during a layover or catching up over Skype after the kids go to bed!

2. **Taking life too seriously!** Remember to laugh with your friends! There are going to be moments and seasons of life that bring challenges with them . . . from surviving final exams to navigating the responsibilities of a new promotion to working through marital conflicts to overcoming an illness to raising a family or losing a loved one. Just because moments are stressful or overwhelming doesn't mean we can't enjoy a good laugh with a friend. In fact, it's our ability to laugh in the face of adversity that gives us the courage to move forward when it would be a lot easier—and feel a lot better—to call it quits!

   Proverbs 17:22 tells us, "A cheerful heart is good medicine." Medical science agrees. Sharing a good laugh with a friend provides numerous benefits. According to licensed massage therapist, Leslie Guerrero Collins, laughing:

   - Lowers blood pressure
   - Increases vascular blood flow and oxygenation of the blood

- Gives a workout to the diaphragm and abdominal, respiratory, facial, leg and back muscles
- Reduces certain stress hormones such as cortisol and adrenaline
- Increases the response of tumor- and disease-killing cells such as Gamma-interferon and T-cells
- Defends against respiratory infections—even reducing the frequency of colds—by immunoglobulin in saliva
- Increases memory and learning
- Improves alertness, creativity and memory[2]

3. **Jealousy.** Nothing kills a friendship faster than jealousy! When we fail to deal with the insecurities in our own souls, we inadvertently sabotage the best of friendships!

   Avoid destructive mind games in which you compare yourself to your friends. When we become jealous of someone else's appearance, talent, opportunity and achievements, we lose the ability to fully love and support our friends. Be confident that God made you wonderfully unique. You are an original, so why try to live as a copy of someone else?

4. **Impatience.** There are no overnight best friends. Think of your closest friendships as being prepared in a crock-pot—simmering for hours and acquiring an

irresistible taste—not in a microwave that pops out a frozen TV dinner in less than three minutes!

The best friendships require T-I-M-E. Don't force a level of intimacy right away; instead, take the time to really get to know someone and allow the friendship to develop into something significant and refreshing!

5. **Disrespect.** When we become too familiar with our friends, it becomes all too easy to forget to communicate honor and respect to one another. Great friendships consist of people who are celebrated and valued. Make sure your words and actions demonstrate kindness, love and respect.

SHIFT HAPPENS

When I (Nicole) was in the second grade, I met my first true girlfriend—my very first BFF. Her name was Jolene. We met in the playground at St. Joseph's Catholic School. We both hated our ugly school uniforms and thought MC Hammer pants were legit! We agreed that Thor Jaramillo was the dreamiest second grader in all of elementary school. We passed funny notes during math class about how weird Father O'Flanagan was. We shared our Fruit Roll-Ups and Cheetos with each other at lunch. We stayed up all night at our sleepovers playing "Truth or Dare" and giggling over boys and silly ghost stories.

Jolene had muscular dystrophy, which left her confined to a wheelchair. In true schoolgirl fashion, we pimped her wheelchair out with Lisa Frank sparkly stickers! Jolene rode around in some serious style! When her electric wheelchair was in the shop for repairs, I would wheel her around our school. I would even run her around our grass field so she could experience what it was like to play goalie in a soccer game. (Granted, we didn't block that many goals, but we had a lot of fun trying!)

Jolene and I were inseparable. She had my back . . . and I had hers. And boy, could we laugh together! I never laughed as hard as I did around Jolene!

One day, toward the end of our fourth grade year, Jolene broke the news to me that her family was moving. One month later, I gave her a homemade goodbye card (with lots of glitter glue and dolphin and puppy stickers on it), and we hugged for the last time. I watched as the U-Haul truck drove off into the distance, taking with it the best friendship any little girl could ask for.

I learned an important and painful lesson that day: Not every friendship will last a lifetime . . . and that's okay.

Some people are in this race with us for the full marathon; others will join us for a mile or two. Some friendships are built for a lifetime; more often than not, friendships shift as seasons in our life change.

It takes wisdom and grace to allow friendships to evolve, and to provide room for friends to grow and change as life goes on.

Friends transfer to out-of-state schools.

They get married.

They move to different neighborhoods.

Their careers take off.

They start families.

Their values and priorities change.

Over time, some close friends may turn into acquaintances. Sometimes, this takes place because of a change in life circumstances (like a move), and sometimes it happens as our values change—we simply "grow apart." As disappointing as this can be, it's a normal part of life. We have to willingly and graciously release people, while always remaining grateful for the role their friendship has played in our lives in seasons past.

SOCIAL MEDIA ETIQUETTE

Back in the day, communicating with friends meant grabbing a cup of coffee at the local coffee shop or chatting on your home phone while folding laundry. Well, those days are long gone! Now we can connect with friends through e-mails, text messages, instant messaging, Facebook, Twitter, Pinterest, Skype . . . to name just a few! With social media comes a whole new list of do's and do-not's. Below are some tips on social media etiquette to help you genuinely connect with friends and avoid some potentially awkward moments along the way!

1. Avoid criticizing someone else, famous or not. Not everyone needs 2 know what u think about Lindsay Lohan's haircut.

2. Stay positive. Posting "My world is falling apart" as an update because a network canceled your favorite TV show may be a little much!

3. No need 2 get political. Express views that r going 2 bring people together . . . not cause a greater divide on hot topics.

4. Please limit photos of your pet 2 once a week. 'Nuff said.

5. A photo that u look cute in, but your friends are making weird faces in . . . doesn't need 2 b posted. & they don't need 2 b tagged either!

6. Do not social media-stalk the cute guy u just met. It's 2 soon 4 u 2 know his every move!

7. Check out the Facebook page of a friend u r getting 2 know or someone u r starting 2 date. U may b surprised! But no stalking! ☻

8. Good rule of thumb: Before posting, ask yourself, "Would I want my grandma 2 view this?"

9. Keep work or school hours 2 actual work or study, & enjoy social media (including checking Facebook) on your lunch break or your own time!

FUN WAYS TO SAY, "LOVE YOU, FRIEND!"

1. Make a "Why My Friend Is So Awesome" list and leave it in her purse for her to find in the middle of the day.

2. Watch her favorite movie with her (for the hundredth time) after she's had a long day. Bonus points if you bring her favorite dessert to share!
3. Give her a ride to the airport, even if it's at 4 A.M. Yikes!
4. Offer to plan her birthday party with a theme that's totally her!
5. Surprise her at work with her favorite latte.
6. Drop off some saltines, ginger ale, chicken soup, and your copy of *The Notebook* at her place when she is stuck at home with the flu.
7. Help her with things that come easily to you but are torture for her: redecorating a room, creating a spreadsheet, buying the perfect black dress . . .
8. Listen to her vent over the phone about her hard day, and offer her encouragement and prayer!

MORE, PLEASE!

(Additional reading)

God Chicks by Holly Wagner

Relationships: How to Make Bad Relationships Better and Good Relationships Great by Drs. Les and Leslie Parrott

Boundaries by Dr. Henry Cloud and Dr. John Townsend

A Garden of Friends by Penny Pierce Rose

Everybody's Normal Till You Get to Know Them by John Ortberg

6

Love Life

HOW TO WIN AT ROMANCE

Love sought is good, but given unsought is better.

WILLIAM SHAKESPEARE

LORD OF YOUR LOVE LIFE?

Growing up, we all imagine our lives will play out like a fairy tale: Our knight in shining armor will rescue us from ever having to be alone, and together we will live happily ever after.

After all, that's what happened to Cinderella, Snow White, Sleeping Beauty and Rapunzel. We've learned from the best.

As we got a little older, our fairy princesses became Kristen Stewart, Katherine Heigl and Rachel McAdams. They were adorable, everyday women who through a series of mishaps and misunderstandings were able to find true love on the big screen in the arms of Robert Pattinson, Ashton Kutcher or Channing Tatum.

They promised us the same happily-ever-after future.

Well, it didn't take us long to realize that all of our beautiful leading ladies had lied. They didn't mean to, but they did.

Skinny jeans have replaced shining armor. Men don't slay dragons; they watch ESPN and don't always know what to say.

In fact, it would seem that men speak an entirely different language than women do. Even worse . . . at times, they aren't charming at all. Sometimes, they are elusive, distant, confusing, or even abusive.

How are we supposed to find the love of our lives in this twenty-first-century world full of reality TV dating shows, STDs, staggering divorce rates, Facebook status changes, and eHarmony?

Well, the good news is that God has His very best in store for YOU! He wants you to enjoy and thrive in every season of life . . . whether you are single, dating, married, or starting a family! His desire is for you to flourish in every area of your life, including romance!

The key to experiencing God's best in your dating life is to make a commitment to honor God when it comes to the choices you make . . . whom you date, how you develop a relationship, and ultimately whom you marry. We win at romance when we go about it God's way! You can trust that when you make Jesus the Lord of your dating life, He will exceed your expectations in the best ways possible! You will discover that God has the right spouse for you at the right time, and together you will live out an expansive life—one that makes an eternal impact and leaves a lasting legacy!

THE SECRET OF CONTENTMENT

I (Nicole) was at a popular café about a month ago, picking up a to-go order. There was a woman in front of me in the to-go line, and a pretty long line of people waiting to order and eat at the café.

I'm pretty sure I only waited five minutes. It was longer than other times, but honestly, not a big deal. It was just five minutes.

But the woman in front of me did not share my spin on the situation . . .

She complained. She mumbled under her breath. She repeatedly looked at her watch. She let out sighs of frustration.

It occurred to me that we were waiting in the same line, but one of us was definitely having a worse time than the other.

I wonder how many times in life we find ourselves huffing and puffing while waiting for something that faith tells us we don't have to worry about. We huff and puff with God about why we haven't been asked out, why all our friends are getting married and starting families, why we don't have more money in the bank, or why we haven't received that promotion at work yet.

Why do we wait that way? Why allow an impatient attitude to sabotage our joy and fulfillment?

Listen to what Paul says about waiting in Philippians 4:11-13:

> I am not saying this because I am in need, for I have learned to be content whatever the circumstances. I know what it is to be in need, and I know what it is to have plenty. I have learned the secret of being content in any and every situation, whether well fed or hungry, whether living in plenty or in want. I can do everything through him who gives me strength.

We can't WAIT well without contentment . . . and the secret to contentment is finding it in Jesus.

Only Jesus can bring us the love, joy, hope, peace and strength that we search for. Only Jesus can fully satisfy our souls.

As long as we keep looking to another person to do in our lives what only Jesus can do, we will always have a sense that "something is missing." If we are not careful, we will look for other things or relationships to fill the void created by our lack of contentment. There is nothing worse than trying to meet a legitimate need in an illegitimate way . . . it will only lead to pain and heartbreak. This might need saying again. There is nothing worse than trying to meet a legitimate need in an illegitimate way . . . it will only lead to pain and heartbreak.

Contentment comes when we stop demanding from people and circumstances what we can only get from Jesus. And what we can get from Jesus—right now, right where we are—is far better than any coffee date, any wedding bells, any pay increase, any job promotion, any career move, or any new home!

PRESS PLAY, NOT PAUSE

Our lives aren't on PAUSE . . . they are happening right now! What God has placed in our hands RIGHT NOW is a grand adventure waiting to be lived. Jesus said He came to give us life and life to the full (see John 10:10).

. . . Not life to the full when you have a boyfriend or wedding or home and 2.5 kids!

There is life to be lived RIGHT NOW!

I talk to so many single people who have great dreams and desires they have put "in storage" until they meet that right someone.

This is our one and only life, and we have a heavenly obligation to live it to the full! Jesus didn't die on a cross because the best possible life He could imagine for us was staying home every night, watching old reruns of *Friends* while downing a pint of Ben & Jerry's. ☻

We were made for much, much more!

What have you been waiting to do? Buy a home, travel to Paris, start that business, learn a new language, go back to school, serve at your local church . . .

Go ahead and do it! Pray and move forward in your purpose and destiny. Don't let dust form on the dreams in your heart. Submit them to Jesus, and pursue wholeheartedly His plans for your life!

THINGS TO DO
- go skydiving
- learn French
- visit Paris and post photos in front of Eiffel Tower on fb
- get my master's degree
- open my home for a church Bible study
- save up for a downpayment on a condo
- road trip with the girls!

WORST PICK-UP LINES EVER!

If a man ever says **ANY** of these things to you with a straight face, please make sure to run in the opposite direction! Then, after you've made your getaway, make sure to have a good laugh with your girlfriends! ☻

1. You must be a thief, because you've stolen my heart.
2. Did it hurt when you fell from heaven?
3. Hey, I've seen you before . . . oh yeah, in my dreams!
4. Baby, you're so sweet, you put Hershey's outta business.
5. Hi, my name's Right . . . as in your Mr. Right.
6. God told me you are the ONE.
7. Do you believe in love at first sight, or should I walk by again?
8. Do you have a map? Because I keep getting lost in your eyes . . .
9. If you were a sandwich at McDonald's, you'd be called McGorgeous!

10. Are your legs tired? 'Cuz you've been running through my mind all night long!

TEN THINGS NOT TO SAY ON A FIRST DATE

1. **"That reminds me of my ex-boyfriend . . . "** (This is not the time to talk about your romantic history!)

2. **"So, when do you see yourself settling down, getting married and having kids?"** (Avoid conversations that lead him to believe you are already picking out the china!)

3. **"I was just wondering . . . how much money do you make exactly?"** (T.M.I., way too soon.)

4. **"Do you have any ibuprofen with you? I have horrible cramps!"** (This is not your girlfriend you are talking to!)

5. **"I was praying, and God told me you are THE ONE."** (That just sounds WEIRD.)

6. **"Do I have something in my teeth?"** (Remember, you are a lady. If you have questions about your appearance, that's what the restroom mirror is for.)

7. **"Let's talk politics! What are your political views?"** (The first date is not the place to debate.)

8. **"It's so great to finally get asked out on a date!"** (And try to leave out any possible references to past Friday nights with Ben & Jerry and the latest romantic comedy.)

9. **"Are you going to open that door for me, or do I have to do everything myself?"** (No one likes a nag.)

10. **"Have you ever thought about getting your eyebrows waxed?"** (Keep all grooming and makeover ideas to yourself.)

TEN THINGS NOT TO DO ON A FIRST DATE

1. **Pile up the garlic.** (Avoid foods that will make your date wish your fascinating conversation were taking place on Skype instead of in person!)

2. **Let loose with your bodily functions.** (Yes, we all get gas, but that doesn't mean we should ask our date to pull our finger or let out a belch after packing down that cheeseburger. Gross!)

3. **Become someone else.** (He asked you out because he likes YOU. You will have some shared interests . . . and some differing ones. You don't have to agree on everything, and you don't need to change your interests just because you like a guy.)

4. **Do all the talking.** (Ask questions. Listen. Make sure that your conversation is two-sided and engaging.)

5. **Text on your phone the whole time.** (There's nothing more annoying than trying to have a meaningful conversation with someone who is too busy texting, checking emails, and posting Twitter updates to pay attention. It's just plain rude.)

6. **Stay out too late.** (Take your time getting to know someone. Even if you are having a great time, it's always a good idea to call it a night at a reasonable hour. Definitely avoid being alone late at night. Like Grandma says, "Nothing good ever happens after 11 P.M.!")

7. **Overanalyze everything.** (It's just coffee. You are getting to know each other. Don't try to figure out if he's the ONE. Take the time to get to know someone, and have fun!)

8. **Forget the other half of that dress at home!** (If you want to be treated like a lady, make sure to dress like one.)

9. **Share too much too soon.** (No one needs to know your whole life story right away. For sure avoid a play-by-play of your dating history. TMI!)

10. **Insist on paying for everything.** (If he asked you out on a date, he wants to be a gentleman! Allow him the opportunity to be chivalrous.)

FOUR WAYS TO LIVE SEXUALLY PURE

God's very best for our lives is to experience the gift of true sexual intimacy inside of marriage. When we choose to honor God with our sexuality, we position ourselves for great blessing and emotional health in both our present dating lives and our future marriages.

Living sexually pure doesn't just happen . . . it takes commitment and intentionality on our part. Below are some thoughts on *avoiding going too far too soon* . . .

1. **Purchase a chastity belt.** (I'm sure you can get a great deal on one on eBay.)

2. **Insist on your father chaperoning all your dates.** (Dad's stink eye will keep

your date on his very best behavior. If he brings his shotgun along for the ride, even better!)

3. **Don't shave your legs.** (Enough said.)

4. **Live stream your dates to your closest friends.** (It'll be your very own reality show, but without the making out in hot tubs.)

Okay, that list was just for fun! But here are *some godly, smart ideas for living sexually pure while in the dating scene . . .*

1. **Set clear boundaries early on in a dating relationship.** (If the man you are dating doesn't share your desire to value purity, then he simply isn't the right guy for you!)

2. **Avoid certain settings.** (You don't need to share the same bed or be alone watching a movie on the couch late at night. Choose to spend the majority of your time in public, safe settings.)

3. **Check in with your friends.** (Make yourself accountable to those close to you. Have them call to find out how a date went. Allow them to ask the tough questions, and be willing to answer honestly.)

4. **Learn from others.** (Seek out the advice and support of women who have successfully navigated living sexually pure, and who have made great decisions in dating.)

PROTECTING THE HEART

Above all else, guard your heart,
for it is the wellspring of life.

PROVERBS 4:23

Your heart is valuable—so valuable, in fact, that it should not be given away to every bidder. You are a daughter of the Most High King, and you are precious in God's sight. Jesus is passionately in love with you . . . so much so that He gave His very life to be with you!

Your heart ought to be protected by wisdom. Make sure that as you get to know and date someone, you make choices that will guard your heart.

One mistake women commonly make in dating is giving their hearts away too freely and too quickly. Make sure to take the time to really get to know the person you are dating.

Don't feel pressured to share the most intimate desires and memories of your heart with someone you barely know. Those aspects of your heart should be reserved for someone who has proven himself trustworthy.

Trust is developed over time.

How does he handle conflict? How does he respond to correction? How does he manage his finances? How does he deal with loss or challenges? How does he treat those closest to him? How does he manage stress?

These are things that can only be discovered over T-I-M-E. Make sure to give more than enough time to really get to know someone before investing your heart in a serious relationship.

We should maintain a slow pace not only emotionally, but also physically. Slowing down physically doesn't just mean abstaining from sex. It also involves being aware of how physically intimate we are early in a relationship. Make sure that your physical interactions—from holding hands to hugging to kissing—develop over time. When physical affection moves too fast, it gives a false sense of closeness that can backfire later on, causing needless heartbreak and confusion.

DRAMA-FREE BREAKUPS

Breaking up is the not-so-fun part of dating. We all know what it feels like to give or receive the "let's just be friends" talk. Awkward, right?

Just because it's uncomfortable doesn't mean it has to be heartbreaking. Through wisdom and humility, we can avoid some of the bad-breakup pitfalls. We recently sat down with Philip Wagner (author, pastor, and the best husband ever!) to get a few tips on achieving drama-free breakups. Here's what he had to say:

Philip Wagner: First off, it's important to keep in mind that not every relationship deserves a "dramatic" breakup.

A simple conversation could be what the relationship calls for. There is a difference between a serious relationship and having gone out on a couple dates. If you've gone out on one or two dates, not getting a call *is* breaking up. But after three or four dates, it's appropriate to have "the talk."

Us: Is it okay to text someone to break up?

Philip Wagner: No. In our world of cell phones, e-mails and texts, it's easier than ever to stay in touch with someone . . . but please, don't use those devices as a way of avoiding confrontation. If you liked a guy enough to kiss him and have a relationship with him, then the very least you can do is honor that connection by ending it in person—face to face. Bottom line: Using technology to break up is cruel and shallow.

Us: Is there a right time or a wrong time to break up?

Philip Wagner: There is never a perfect time, but it's good to be thoughtful about what is going on in the other person's life. You don't want to put it off too long, but if your boyfriend is already going through a difficult time—say he lost his job yesterday, or a family crisis came up—it can wait a week or two. If there's a special occasion like a birthday or Christmas . . . again, it can wait a week.

Us: How long should the conversation last?

Philip Wagner: Give the person a fair amount of time to process the breakup. You probably want to deliver the news and then get the heck out of there . . . but don't be in such a hurry. It's really unfair to tell him without giving him adequate time to process.

Us: What if he tries to talk you into changing your mind?

Philip Wagner: That happens sometimes. You might have to endure some tears, hear about some frustrations, or even bear some accusations out of hurt . . . but talking about it is the right thing to do. It's important to give him the chance to ask questions and feel the sentiment behind your words. If he gets upset, cries or even gets angry—don't try to stop him. Guys are allowed to have and express feelings. Keep in mind, you've been thinking about the breakup for a few days; he only heard about it a couple minutes ago. But if at any point you feel threatened, or he gets overly aggressive, leave immediately and let him know you are willing to talk later, when he has calmed down.

Us: Are there certain things that shouldn't be said during a breakup?

Philip Wagner: For one, this is not the place to criticize him or place blame on him. Also, please don't say, "It's not you, it's me" or "God told me to break up with you." Simply stick to clarifying YOUR feelings and YOUR decisions. Make sure to take some time to reassure him and affirm the significance he has had in your life.

If he asks for reasons for the breakup, don't be hurtful. Avoid unnecessary insults and criticisms. Instead, your reasons for the split should focus on how the two of you aren't a good match for each other.

Finally, please don't give false hope about the future just to make him feel better in the moment. Giving people a false sense of hope doesn't help or heal them.

Us: This has been so insightful! Any last tips on drama-free breakups?

Philip Wagner: To the best of your ability, speak highly of your ex after the breakup, and allow some distance between you and him. It might be okay to agree to keep in touch, but not usually. Recognize that more than likely you will be "acquaintances" in the future. Depending on the seriousness of the relationship you just ended, don't jump right into another one. You may need to take time to heal, recover, and grow in your relationship with Jesus before entering into a new relationship.

WHOM TO TAKE HOME TO MOM AND DAD

One of the most important decisions we will ever make is whom we marry. Whom we choose as a spouse will affect us much more than a career choice or schooling or even our friendships. With that in mind, how do we know whom to get serious with? What qualities should we look for in someone we'll be bringing home to meet Mom and Dad?

1. **A man who is a committed follower of Jesus.** This is number one on the list for a reason! Make sure to invest in a relationship with someone who has a sincere and genuine faith in Jesus! His relationship with Jesus should inspire and encourage you in yours!

   We're not just talking about someone who calls himself a Christian, but someone who consistently makes choices that honor God and His plans for his life.

   Remember, you will never have to forfeit the call of God on your life in order to marry someone. You will never have to compromise your relationship with Jesus in order to invest in a dating relationship. And you never even have to entertain the thought of dating someone who doesn't have the same faith in Jesus that you have!

2. **A man who knows how to communicate honor and respect.** Look for someone who considers your

desires and feelings before making decisions. He should demonstrate respect in his treatment of you and others around him, as well as in how he talks to and about others.

Someone who really respects you will honor the purposes of God in your life! He will support you and encourage you to pursue wholeheartedly the great plans God has for you, and won't be intimidated by your dreams for the future!

3. **A man who is protective about you and your feelings.** He should be considerate of you and do his best to care for and support you. Under pressure, he should demonstrate an ability and willingness to look out for you. This means that he conducts his dating relationship with you in a way that is protective of your emotional and spiritual well-being. He should date you in such a way that it doesn't jeopardize you, your family life, your friendships, and most importantly, your relationship with Jesus.

4. **A man who serves others.** In today's culture, it is pretty easy to become self-focused. Make sure to partner with someone who can see beyond his own needs and is committed to addressing others' needs. Is he serving in your local church? Is he quick to help out you and his friends? Is he generous with his

time and his resources? Great marriages are developed when both husband and wife are committed to serving each other. Look for someone who is actively serving others now.

5. **A man with vision.** He should have direction for his life and a strong desire to make a real difference in the world. A lot of people have dreams for their futures, but the man you are dating should have more than a dream . . . he should be taking real steps toward those dreams! Ultimately, you want to be in a serious relationship with a man who is passionately and ambitiously pursuing God's will for his life!

HE'S NOT YOUR GIRLFRIEND

You don't have to be a rocket scientist to realize that men and women communicate very differently. For one, we women tend to have more words in our daily quota than men ever will! We also tend to connect more easily with people through communication. It's how God wired us.

It may be true that men need help learning how to communicate their feelings, but even with that help, they will likely never communicate like women!

That's a good thing. God made men and women different to complement each other.

If we are going to have meaningful relationships with men, we have to learn to communicate in a way that men understand and that makes them feel valued.

In other words, we need to remember that our boyfriends aren't our girlfriends! If we try to talk to men like we do to our girlfriends, we will find ourselves running into a lot of cement walls in the communication department.

With that in mind, here are a few ways to improve communication with your boyfriend:

- **Use fewer words.** Men tend to be direct. They will have an easier time actively listening to the 3-minute description of your day at work than the 30-minute version.

- **Ease up on the subtleties.** Dropping hints is an art form for women. That's not the case for men! Don't expect them to know what you're thinking. Instead, be clear about what you are asking of them or feeling.

- **Realize that your delivery matters.** It's not just what you say, but how you say it. Your tone will communicate either honor and respect or disrespect and frustration. Make sure to approach discussions with a tone that communicates that you value him, even if you are disagreeing about something.

- **Show your appreciation.** Thank him for specific kind and admirable things he has done, and make sure to let him know how those things made you feel. Men want to know that they aren't just tolerated, but celebrated! Encourage his efforts to care for and support you. When you are your partner's biggest cheerleader, you help him grow as a man of character and strength.

- **Do more listening.** Get to know his interests. Understand how he is feeling and how you can support him. Ask questions about him as you continue to date. Let him know you want to keep learning more about him. When you find yourself in a conflict, fight fair. Actually listen to his side of things and discover his perspective.

MORE, PLEASE!

(Additional reading)

GodChicks and the Men They Love by Philip and Holly Wagner

Date . . . or Soul Mate? by Neil Clark Warren, Ph.D.

Boundaries in Dating by Dr. Henry Cloud and Dr. John Townsend

Your Knight in Shining Armor by P. B. Wilson

The Purity Principle by Randy Alcorn

7

Tying the Knot

BUILDING A MARRIAGE THAT LASTS

There is no more lovely, friendly, and charming relationship, communion or company than a good marriage.

MARTIN LUTHER

CINDERELLA LIED!

I (Holly) loved Philip. He loved me.

Then we said, "I do."

Like Cinderella, I thought that was all it took to get to happily ever after—love and a wedding ring.

Uhhh . . . she lied.

Thinking that marriage is as simple as love, a wedding ring, and the right house is about as naive as thinking that all you have to do to get great abs is want them and buy a cute workout outfit! Sadly, great abs come after lots of crunches, Pilates and diet control.

Just like marriage.

Well . . . maybe not the Pilates . . . but definitely the work.

Don't worry—it is not a life sentence of hard labor! It is work to bring enjoyment!

But yes . . . building relationships is a lot of work.

Period.

I don't know anyone who has been married very long who will not attest to that.

Great marriages are not genetic. They don't happen just because you want one or hope to have one. If that were true, everyone everywhere would have a great marriage. The desire for a healthy marriage is really only the first step on a long list of steps. Sadly, many couples don't make it very far down the list.

It's good to remember that struggling marriages don't just happen either.

There are a lot of reasons for divorce.

Communication breakdown.

Personality differences.

Sexual frustration or unfaithfulness.

Money problems.

Unresolved issues of the past.

It can't just be your spouse that is the problem (although there are days when I am convinced he is . . .). Sometimes we think that if we were just married to someone else, then our problems would be solved.

Not so.

Sixty percent of second marriages end in divorce too.[1]

I have heard that divorce statistics for third and fourth marriages are even higher.

Maybe at the core of all of these numbers is a lack of preparation. Most of us spend more time planning for the wedding than we do for the marriage.

How much time do we spend on the selection of wedding invitations . . . flowers . . . meals . . . a wedding dress . . . ? We agonize over how many bridesmaids to have . . . where to hold the ceremony . . . our honeymoon plans . . . and so on and so forth.

I am not saying that you shouldn't plan your big day . . . but really, if we just spent as much time preparing for the commitment of marriage as we do for our wedding day, then our marriages would start off much healthier.

We expect our physicians to have gone through years of school and residency in order to be good at what they do, yet most of us expect to have a strong marriage without ever learning how. Wouldn't it be great if all universities required students to take a Marriage 101 class? In the long run, that class would probably prove more useful than the calculus class I took! But even for those of us who missed the Marriage 101 class, there is hope!

For those of you who are planning a wedding . . . how about working on these things too . . .

Is your passion for Jesus the same?

How will you handle finances?

What are your expectations in terms of husband/wife roles?

Do you both want children?

How do you handle disagreements?

How much will your in-laws have to do with your marriage?

What will you do during leisure time?

Are you both equally committed to a church?

FIGHTING THE "YOU COMPLETE ME" SYNDROME

In the movie *Jerry McGuire,* Tom Cruise's character says to the love of his life, "You complete me." Now, that certainly sounds romantic, and like the other women watching the movie, we probably all said "*Awwww!*" when we heard it. But honestly, that is nonsense.

We shouldn't be looking for someone to complete us.

You are not some fragmented being looking for a man to fill the gaps. God didn't create you as a half. A healthy relationship is when two wholes come together . . . so the goal is for each of us to be whole before joining our life to someone else's.

When God told Adam that it wasn't good for him to be alone (see Gen. 2:18), the woman was created to bring partnership. She was created to add to his life, not take away from it.

Solomon said that two are better than one (see Eccles. 4:9).

Doing the math, we know that 1 + 1 = 2.

By contrast, 1/2 + 1/2 = 1, which is not better than one. Two whole people can engage in a mutually dependent relationship—with honest, open and vulnerable communication and accountability—while encouraging and urging each other further and deeper into the purpose of God.

Two halves united together will typically experience false intimacy laced with veins of co-dependency, secrets, hiding, miscommunication and fear. When it comes to each other's purpose and destiny . . . well, it is very hard to encourage your mate to become who they are meant to be in God, when you aren't even sure who you are in Him.

You are designed to bring help and companionship to the relationship.

Together, you and your husband will accomplish far more than either of you could alone.

A positive self-image is vital, but remember that my ability to like myself does not come simply from thinking that I am wonderful. It comes from knowing that God thinks that (see Ps. 139:14).

I am His masterpiece (see Eph. 2:10).

His one-of-a-kind creation.

The deepest needs of my soul can only be met by my Creator—and they will be if I have an honest and real relationship with Him.

We have to quit asking our husbands to meet needs that only God can.

Neediness demands. Having a need, asks.

Most of us fall into one of the following categories:

1. **Independent** (we think we can do everything on our own—or at least, we try to)

   Not good, because we are designed to do life together.

2. **Dependent** (fully relying on someone, as an infant would a mother)

   Not good, because God is the only one who can be our All-sufficiency. Our spouses cannot fill that role.

3. **Interdependent** (confident in ourselves, and yet needing others to fulfill our purpose)

   Good, because we were designed for reciprocal relationships that are rooted in God.

SEVEN RULES FOR FIGHTING FAIR

(These work for any relationship . . . not just marriage!)

Wouldn't it be easier if all of life were like the climate control in a car? The car we have has dual controls, so I can make it cooler or warmer on my side of the car, and Philip can have his side how he wants it. I can even warm up my seat, and he can make his cool. Pretty awesome! Sometimes I wish life could be full of "his and her" everything, but it isn't. Most of the time, the conflict we experience in marriage arises because we are not willing to give up what we want.

I have a friend who was raised in a family whose way to resolve any conflict was to fight it out. Just fight until you win. These were not necessarily physical fights, but definitely verbal fights that got louder and louder. One person always had to win, and the other was made to feel totally wrong. There was either complete domination or complete submission—no compromising or meeting in the middle.

Surely this is not the best way.

Then I have talked to people who were raised in families where one or both parents backed down from anything resembling a confrontation—they would just give in, totally avoiding any conflict whatsoever. One of my friends who grew up in this kind of environment said that this method of dealing with conflict kept the peace for a while, but eventually there would be an explosion.

That way can't be good either.

There are right and wrong ways to face and resolve conflict.

I am not a big fan of boxing, but I do know that there are rules in boxing. There are rules in karate. There are rules in wrestling. I am not sure about the WWE or Lucha Libre (made famous in the movie *Nacho Libre*) . . . but I think that, even in those matches, there are a few basic ground rules.

Rule #1: The first step toward resolving conflict is to make sure that you yourself are at peace with God.

It sounds so basic, but we were created to have a relationship with Him, and our ability to connect with people comes out of our relationship with God. I just don't think that we will ever have peace with people if we haven't made our peace with God. Sometimes conflict occurs because we are expecting people—in this case, our husbands—to meet needs that only God can meet. As amazing as your husband is—and he is amazing—he is not your Savior. He has nothing with which to save you.

Rule #2: Ask God how much of this problem might be your fault.

Before you attack or accuse or blame, check yourself out. Jesus said that before we worry about that little piece of sawdust in somebody else's eye, we should remove the tree trunks from our own eyes (see Matt. 7:3). We all have tree trunks in our eyes sometimes. We can all get so focused on the weaknesses and faults of the other that we forget we have shortcomings of our own. The reality is, some part of the conflict is my fault, and the responsibility for that part of the problem is 100 percent mine. I have to own that.

So now, occasionally I will ask myself questions like, *Am I being oversensitive? Am I being insensitive? Am I being ungrateful or too demanding?* Oftentimes, if I am honest, the answer to one of those questions is yes—which means that I have to take responsibility for what I have contributed to the conflict.

Rule #3: (This is the tough part.) Apologize for your part of the problem first.

Get great at saying, "I'm sorry."

Not, "I'm sorry, but . . ."

Just "I'm sorry for being oversensitive." Or too demanding . . . or whatever.

Maybe, just maybe, you are wrong in this instance. I am sure he needs to apologize, too. He undoubtedly has a tree trunk in his own eye. But you can only deal with you, so I am saying be 100 percent responsible for your part.

Apologizing does not mean that the issue is over; it just means that there is now the right atmosphere for solving whatever the conflict might be.

Rule #4: Trying to see an issue from the other's point of view is important.

It is not always easy, because the only perspective from which we naturally see life is our own. A number of years ago, Philip and I were looking for a house.

This was when I was still living under the illusion that all men knew how to fix things . . . or could manage people who knew how to fix things. We walked into a house that was for sale. It was the funkiest house ever, and I just loved it. It had a tree growing right in the middle of it. The previous owner had begun some renovations, laying the groundwork for what I thought would be the most amazing house.

As I walked around the house, I said things like, "We could put this here, and do that there. In this room we could do this." As Philip walked through it, he saw all the work that would need to be done—none of which he had any idea how to do. In his mind, he saw months of sawdust, hammers and chaos. I got frustrated with him as he let me know we were not going to live in that house. I said things like, "Why do we always have to do things your way? Why can't we have a house like this?"

I remember walking off by myself and really trying to see the situation from his perspective. He wanted a home—a peaceful home. He had no idea how to create a peaceful home out of this half-finished building. I came to recognize and understand the stress that even the thought of living there gave him.

So we walked away from that house that needed lots of work . . . and eventually moved into a beautiful home that only required us to unpack our boxes and mount a lamp. Perfect! Working hard at trying to see the issue from his point of view helped resolve that particular conflict.

It's amazing how well this approach works—not only with husbands, but also with friends.

Work hard at trying to see issues from your loved one's point of view and watch those conflicts begin to resolve.

Rule #5: You will need to pick a time to resolve the issue.

Timing is key. For instance, on the way to his birthday party is probably **not** the time to let your husband know that he could lose a few pounds. (Wish I could tell you I learned that from a book!) Now, the issue may have been a fair one to bring up, but the timing was not good. If his mom just got diagnosed with Alzheimer's, it's probably not the time to tell him you think he should read a book on parenting. Again, the issue may be a reasonable one to bring up . . . the timing is just wrong.

Is it late at night?
Has he had a long day?

Is he at work?
Maybe those would not be the best times to start a difficult conversation.

If you are trying to resolve conflict with a friend . . . consider the timing as well.
Has she just been in the hospital with one of her parents?
Is her child having a crisis?
Is her house flooded?
You get the idea.

We need to be sensitive to whether or not this is the right time to bring up the issue. The goal is to resolve the problem at hand, not create another one.

Rule #6: Picking the right place is also important. Running out the door on the way somewhere is probably not the place to resolve anything. Because neither one of you will feel like you are heard, and you will feel like you need to hurry through the process. The place to work out an issue is away from the telephone and other distractions.

The bed is probably not the place to work out the issue either, because any man left horizontal for long will start snoring! (This will just cause another issue that will need to be resolved!) Besides, a couple's bed shouldn't be a place of conflict. It should be a place for intimacy. You don't want to bring a fight there.

Taking a walk can be a great place to resolve issues. Or over coffee at Starbucks. Or sitting by the beach. Or hiking in the woods. Or on a park bench. You pick a place that works for you.

Rule #7: Words matter. There are some verbal weapons that Philip and I have agreed never to use against each other. For example, we have decided that no matter what kind of conflict we get into, we will never use the word "divorce." Ever. If divorce is not an option, then we realize that working things out is the only solution.

Think about the damage you may cause before you launch that verbal missile. Sadly, sometimes my method is *Ready . . . Fire . . . Aim.* Not good! Reckless shooting can cause damage that is impossible to fix. Words cannot be taken back . . . only forgiven.

I love M&Ms, especially the peanut ones. Back when I used to eat that kind of stuff, I could polish off a bag really quickly . . . in about 35 seconds! It only took

35 seconds to consume a bag full of fat and sugar . . . and it would take about 30 minutes of exercise to work off all those calories—not to mention the hours that my body would require to get rid of the toxins I had ingested.

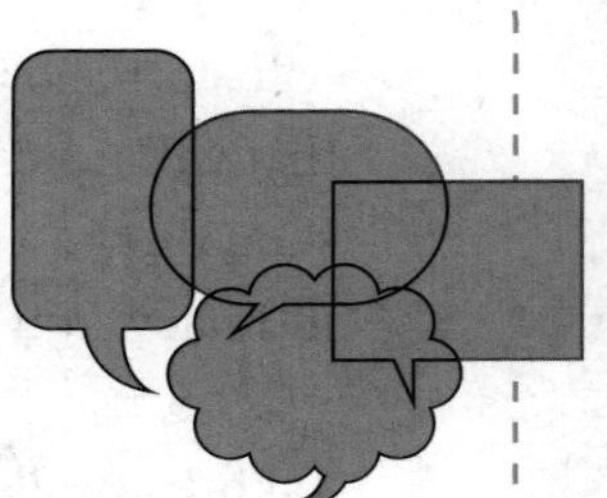

This is like a verbal missile . . . we can throw one at our partner in a matter of seconds, but it may take years to work off the damage.

Besides "divorce," Philip and I try to refrain from using words like "never" or "always"—because they are rarely true. "We *never* do anything I want to do!" "You *always* ignore me!" "You *never* think about me!" "You *never* say that you love me!" Nobody "always" or "never" does anything, so be careful about using these absolute words.

To these seven rules, add the basic ones you probably learned in kindergarten: No yelling. No pushing. No hitting. No kicking. No biting. No slamming doors.

CLASS IN SESSION: QUESTIONS TO ASK

Whether preparing for marriage or seeking to deepen your relationship with your husband, it's always important to ask questions.

Questions are a great way to get to know someone (and to continue to learn about someone you already know well).

How about you? Are you asking questions?

Try these:

"What is your biggest fear?"

"What do you want our life to look like in five years?"

"If you had a million dollars, what would you do with it?"

"What are two things you love about me?"

"If money were no object, where would you like to go on vacation?"

"What are you looking forward to?"

"What makes you feel the most alive?"

Over the years, the questions might change, but we should still ask them. The answers might change, too. Because the truth is . . . both you and your husband are mysteries that will never be completely solved.

A stale marriage occurs when no one cares enough to ask questions. When we quit learning about each other.

Dr. Robin Smith, in her book *Lies at the Altar*, suggests 276 questions that should be asked before marriage . . . and asked again during marriage. They should be answered truthfully . . .

not how you think your partner wants you to answer them. After all, it is truth that sets us free!

If you are dating and you don't have the time to ask the questions, then you don't have the time to get married.

Here are a few of the questions Dr. Smith suggests:

- Are you working in your chosen profession?
- How many hours a week do you work?
- Do you prefer urban, suburban or rural settings?
- Do you think of your home as a cocoon, or is your door always open?
- If you had unlimited resources, how would you live?
- Do you have any debts?
- When was the first time you felt that you were in love with another person?
- Do you exercise regularly?
- What do you like or dislike about your appearance?
- Do you want children?

- Have you ever been alienated from your family?
- Do you have a best friend?
- Are you serving in church?
- What is your idea of a fun day?
- Do you enjoy traveling?
- Do you like to cook? Eat?
- Are there household responsibilities that you think are primarily male or female?
- Are you a morning person or night person?[2]

Being a perpetual student is crucial. (Not that you need to remain in college forever—please don't.) Please continue to learn new things . . . about life and your spouse . . . and then do the work necessary to put what you have learned into practice.

No matter how long we have been married, we all need to remain students in our marriages.

Why is it that we often spend more time and effort becoming better at our jobs or careers—which may or may not last a decade—than we do learning about, and becoming better at, marriage?

Being a wife is a role you will have for many years, so dedicate yourself to learning and growing in it.

We all learned in biology class that the way to tell a living organism from an inanimate one is by observing any change. After a time, if there is no growth or change, the object is considered to be dead.

The same is true with you and me as individuals and as part of a couple.

We must grow.

As individuals, we must be willing to learn new things and think new thoughts. If we are thinking only the same old thoughts, we won't make it through life the way we are supposed to. We need to meet new people, read new books, take on new challenges, and set new goals.

Basically, we need to be lifelong students.

As part of a marriage, I had to grow in a few ways. Primarily, I had to truly become a student of Philip—not only in recognizing his personality strengths and weaknesses, but also in learning his likes, dislikes and needs. From the simple to the more complex—from remembering his favorite food to knowing what he needs when he is hurting—I had a lot to learn. Then, I had to be willing for him to change his mind . . . which meant I had to learn new stuff all over again! The tricky thing for me was learning about him . . . not to change him . . . but to know him.

Some people come crying to a counselor: "He's not the same person I married!" Well, probably not . . . and neither are you. Our tastes, interests and emotional needs change over time. That's what keeps life and relationships interesting, and why we have to continue to be students.

Maybe he needs time to process most things.

Or maybe he likes the computer and television on when he is reading. Perhaps he doesn't like human interruptions when he is studying.

Maybe he is not a big fan of surprises.

Or perhaps he takes his time when making decisions.

Maybe he doesn't like interjections when he is talking. (Maybe he actually calls them interruptions.)

Maybe he reads multiple books at the same time, not always completely finishing any of them.

What if the first thing he wants to do in the morning is turn on his computer?

Do you know that he doesn't like long meals in fancy restaurants?

Now, what if you are completely the opposite in every one of those areas? That can make a marriage challenging! If we're honest, sometimes deep in our hearts, we wish our husbands were more like us . . . and that's not good! Because it means that you have stopped studying who he is, and instead are focusing on who you want him to be.

TEN WAYS TO LOVE YOUR HUSBAND

1. **Be kind.** Most of the time, we are kinder and more polite to strangers and acquaintances than we are to our spouses. It should not be that way, but often it is. Little acts of kindness can go a long way toward creating intimacy.

2. **Demonstrate respect.** You are not his mother, so don't talk down to him or nag him. Interrupting him communicates disrespect (at least, that is what Philip tells me!). So, let him finish his sentences . . . no matter how good you think your ending would be!

3. **Get some sexy lingerie.** Enough said, really.

4. **Occasionally be the sexual aggressor.** He likes/needs to feel that you want him. Don't just be the passive one. Mix it up!

5. **Go with him to a game/sporting event.** He really does want your company. It is not about whether or not you like sports—just doing something with him shows your love. (But you are a smart woman, so surely you can learn a thing or two about the sport while you're at it!)

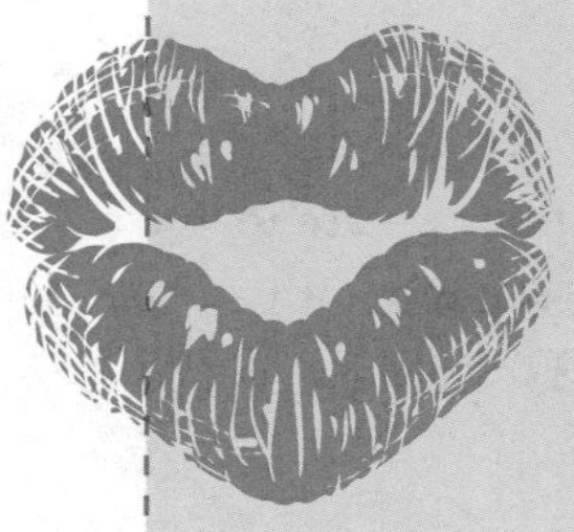

6. **Kiss him.** I'm not talking about the quick "don't mess up my lipstick" kiss, but the "stop and grab his face" kiss. Even if you don't have time for it to lead anywhere ☻ . . . kissing is such a great connector!

7. **Listen without interrupting.** Yes, I know this one is hard . . .

8. **Encourage him.** Say something encouraging to him. He probably hears negativity all day long from others. What can you say that would be encouraging? What has he done well? Be his biggest cheerleader!!

9. **Say nice things about him in front of others.** This is huge . . . and communicates love in a whole other way.

10. **Show support for his dreams.** Come alongside him and support him. Life has a way of deflating our dreams. Let him know that you are with him and believe in him.

WHAT YOUR MOMMA DIDN'T TELL YOU ABOUT SEX

Great sex is not about how many people you can have intercourse with, but rather the intimacy that occurs in a marriage when two committed people join hearts and bodies. This kind of intimacy grows over the years.

Sex should be fun. We should both experience physical pleasure and touch each other emotionally at a deep level. The average person thinks that Christians are uptight and sexually repressed simply because we have convictions we believe should guide us. But emotionally and sexually healthy Christians experience passionate, uninhibited, hot, laugh-out-loud, heart-stopping and jaw-dropping sex!!!

INGREDIENTS FOR GREAT SEX

1. **Developing good communication.** We have to be willing to discuss our thoughts, fears and feelings. We have to be willing to talk about what we like and what we don't like. And we must be willing to listen without being insecure or rejecting the desires and concerns of our mates.

2. **Honesty.** Honesty is another tool. It's important that we ask (and truthfully answer) questions like . . . "What have I done that you like?" . . . "What have I done that you don't like?" . . . "What makes you uncomfortable?" . . . "In what ways can I touch you that would be arousing?" Questions like these can go a long way toward building understanding and unity.

3. **Being willing to learn, change and grow.** It takes work to have a great sex life. (Or maybe instead of thinking of it as work, we should see it as an investment in our marriage!) If you want to have a better sex life than you do now, you're going to have to change. There is more to learn about sex . . . yes, even for you. Sometimes we act like we know what we're doing, but how would we know if we've never discussed these intimate issues with our spouses?

4. **Keeping a sense of humor**. The best way to break tension is to laugh—not at each other or at the attempts to please . . . but just at the humorous situations that can arise. Relax. Playfulness is part of a great sex life. You can't take yourself so seriously. You have to laugh a little and play a little. This is an enjoyable part of life. You get to learn. You get to practice again and again. Sometimes you get it right and sometimes . . . not so much . . . but you get to try it again tomorrow!

5. **Creativity and imagination.** Eating the same thing for dinner every night would quickly get boring, no matter how good it tasted. In the same way, your sex life might get a bit humdrum if you do not apply your God-given creativity to it.

   In today's culture, to promote "creativity," couples are sometimes encouraged to bring pornography—via movies or the Internet—into the bedroom. This is NOT the kind of creativity we mean. Bringing someone else into the bed, even if only on film, will eventually undermine the work you and your husband are doing to become one.

   There are plenty of other ways to be creative—just the two of you. Whether it is turning the music on and dancing in the bedroom, or you wearing a sexy dress to catch his eye . . . the ideas are endless. We are not going to tell you how to be creative . . . just that you need to be. Whatever ideas you come up with should be things that both of you are comfortable with and enjoy.

It is possible in today's society to build a strong marriage. It really can be done. That said, there will be seasons in a marriage that are more difficult than others.

The season when you have young children who seem to take up all of your time. Don't lose sight of the marriage.

The season when you want children, but can't seem to get pregnant. Don't lose sight of the marriage.

The season of trying to work around two careers, school and a family. Don't lose sight of the marriage.

Philip and I have been married for 27 years, and there were moments in the early years when I wanted out. My bags were packed, and I was leaving. All I can say is: I am so glad I didn't. We really are enjoying the sweet years now. I am more in love with him than I ever have been. So don't give up. Really.

MORE, PLEASE!

(Additional reading)

GodChicks and the Men They Love by Philip and Holly Wagner

Love and Respect by Dr. Emerson Eggerichs

The Triumphant Marriage by Neil Clark Warren, Ph.D.

Creating an Intimate Marriage by Jim Burns

8

Modern Family

HOW TO MAINTAIN A HEALTHY HOUSEHOLD

Before I got married I had six theories about bringing up children; now I have six children and no theories.

JOHN WILMOT, EARL OF ROCHESTER

A few years ago, I (Holly) visited Seaside, Florida, which has to be the most perfect-looking town I have ever seen. People in this master planned community, whether visitors or residents, rode bicycles along the perfectly groomed sidewalks . . . to the perfectly clean Starbucks, to the perfect-looking stores, to the perfectly designed school, to the perfectly adorable post office, to the perfect ice cream parlor, to the perfectly beautiful chapel, to the perfect-looking grocery store, to the perfect restaurants, to the perfectly sandy beach, and then back to their perfect-looking homes.

As someone coming from the city of Los Angeles, which is far from perfect-looking, I found this experience to be quite novel. Riding around on my bicycle in this perfect town, I felt like I was on a movie set. In fact, I was. Seaside, Florida, was the community used in the filming of the movie *The Truman Show.* If you have seen the film, you'll recall that it tells the story of a man who was unaware he was living in a totally controlled environment.

However, unlike Truman, we don't live in a bubble.

Our families must figure out how not only to exist, but also to thrive, in the real world, with all of its distractions and complications. Most of us do not live on some remote desert island where we get to focus entirely on one another 24 hours a day. Nope. We have to work out our marriages and our families with all the trappings that come with life in the twenty-first century.

How do we do that and not lose sight of each other?

PAST, PRESENT . . . FUTURE!

We do bring our pasts—good and bad—into our marriages. Each of us enters adulthood with a different background, and those backgrounds will have an effect on our marriage, often feeling like a third person invading our present.

My friend Priscilla Shirer (I call her "my sista from anotha mista") was one of the speakers at our GodChicks conference in 2008. She told a great story that has stuck with me. She and her husband, Jerry, went to minister to a local church. When they arrived, a little exhausted from the weeks leading up to this visit, they were grateful to settle into their hotel and looked forward to getting some rest.

However, they were awakened in a panic around 11 P.M. by the sound of a train whistling past their room. After their near heart attack, they fell back asleep . . . only to be awakened again by the same sound at 1 A.M. . . . and then again at 5:30 in the morning. So much for resting!

When a woman from the church arrived the next morning to drive them to the meeting, Priscilla gently mentioned that the loudest train on the entire planet had kept them up throughout the entire night.

The girl's face turned white as a sheet. She began to apologize profusely and then explained that the people who had been living in the town for years could no longer even hear the train as it went by.

I'd like to suggest that many of us are the same way. We get so used to the voices of our pasts whistling around in our minds that we don't even notice them anymore. We can live with depression, insecurity, jealousy, self-loathing, lust or pride for so long that we no longer recognize their daily impact on our lives.

When another person enters our environment, the voice we have learned to live with is incredibly loud to our partner and may continuously disrupt his rest . . . like the train disrupted Priscilla and Jerry's.

In marriage, hidden issues will come out of hiding. In the light of another's perspective, we will be forced to face our problem areas. Because our spouses don't share our exact struggles, things we have learned to ignore or accommodate will sound like a roaring train to them . . . this is the third person from the past invading our present.

Maybe we had parents who loved us and loved each other, so we are confident in relationships. But there are a lot of us who have been hurt and betrayed . . . and aren't quite so secure in building relationships.

Maybe you experienced years of abuse and are now on a healing journey . . . but it is a journey . . . and your husband will have to be patient while you walk it out. There will be times when your past will interfere with your present. That can be frustrating, and you both have to remain focused on what you are building together.

Maybe he was raised by a single mother and really has no idea what a husband . . . much less a father . . . should do. When you marry him, you are committing to encouraging him on that journey . . . and joining him in working through the frustrations that come with it.

Maybe he expects a home-cooked meal because that's how his mom did it . . . but you have never even been in a kitchen. Maybe you expect him to fix whatever breaks around the house . . . but he has never even held a hammer. Our pasts, along with the expectations that come from them, will enter into the reality of our marriage. So be prepared to deal with them together.

Often our pasts will include a relationship or two (or more). Philip was not the first person to ask me to marry him. He is just the only one to whom I said "I do."

So, like most of us, I came into my marriage with a past. Not a sordid one, because the truth is I only dated great guys. I never spent any time with any man who did not treat me with respect and kindness.

You know that saying that you have to kiss a lot of frogs before one becomes a prince? Not true . . . I kissed no frogs. I wasted no time with frogs. Honestly, I only have great memories of the men I dated before I met Philip.

But that can be a problem, too. In the first few years of our marriage, whenever Philip would make me mad, my head would be full of thoughts of a past boyfriend whom, in that moment, I could only remember as being perfect. I would think, *I should have stayed with ______. He wouldn't be treating me this way.* Also not true. I had said no to that guy for a reason.

We can't prevent our pasts from having an influence on our marriage. But it is crucial that we watch where our thoughts lead us. Keep your focus on today. Stay engaged in this relationship that you are building.

HOME FOR THE HOLIDAYS?!

Some of you love the thought of Christmas approaching. You delight in the anticipation, the shopping, the meals and the family time. Others of you dread the whole season, wishing the calendar would quickly turn from the day before Thanksgiving to January 2. Most of our feelings about Christmas come from our memories of childhood Christmases.

Here's the thing.

You are not a child anymore. If you have great memories of Christmas, it is because someone made your Christmas great. Now you are the grownup. It is your turn to make Christmas great for someone else.

If you have painful holiday memories, then it is now your turn to create new ones.

Be careful about getting sentimental.

Be careful about wasting time wishing your memories were different.

Going to visit your family for Christmas can be a good thing . . . and it can be a painful time.

If going to see your family only brings you pain . . . why go? If you keep hoping that your dad won't get drunk this time, or your mom won't constantly berate you, then maybe you should stay away. Or at least keep your visit brief.

As a grownup, you get to make your own traditions.

If you are married, you have a new family . . . and you get to create your own holiday memories.

FIVE HOLIDAY TRADITIONS TO CONSIDER

1. Attend a candlelight service
2. Have a special Christmas breakfast

3. Read the story of Jesus' birth before you open gifts
4. Invite friends to Christmas dinner
5. Go see a movie Christmas night

FOR THOSE OF YOU WITH CHILDREN: TWELVE WAYS TO MANAGE LIFE AND PICK UP KIDS FROM SOCCER PRACTICE ON TIME

1. Post a calendar somewhere in your house so that everyone knows who is going where.
2. Trade babysitting with other parents.

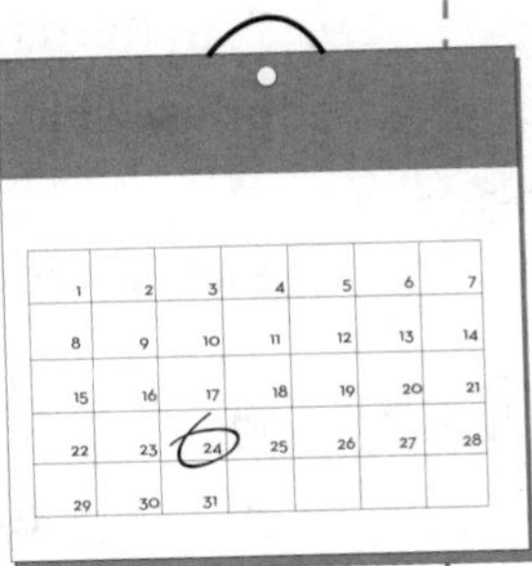

3. Keep dinner simple. Especially if both parents work outside the home, this can be a challenging hour. But it doesn't have to be. The point is to have a meal together . . . not to impress your gourmet neighbor.
4. Get school clothes and lunches ready the night before.

5. Do a lot of laughing. For instance, when your third-grade son tells you that his science project is due tomorrow and he hasn't even started it . . .

6. Get up earlier in the morning. Even a few extra minutes will help because something always comes up. Rushing around and that feeling of "running late" cause stress for everyone.

7. Limit the number of teams and after-school activities your kids are involved in. They can't do everything at the same time . . . and neither can you.

8. Carpool with other families.

9. Plan the days of the week that the house gets cleaned, or on which day which part gets done.

10. Plan a laundry day . . . or two or four or even six! ☻

11. Plan meals in advance, maybe a week at a time, so that trips to the grocery are minimized and advance preparations can be made. If it is a freezable meal, then make double and freeze one.

12. Forgive yourself when you don't get it right!

SIX ORGANIZATIONAL TIPS (SO YOU DON'T END UP ON *HOARDERS!*)

1. Have a landing strip. This is the bowl or tray that you put everything in when you come home. That way you are not always looking for your keys, phone and other pocket-sized belongings.

2. Clean as you go. Really. Makes all the difference.

3. Everything in its place.

4. If your house is currently an organizational nightmare . . . start small. One room at a time. You can do it!

5. Use a calendar. Either the paper kind or an online version will work . . . as long as you remember to use it!!

6. How many things do you really need to collect??? Most of them just become "dust catchers."

EIGHT WAYS TO CLEAN YOUR HOUSE QUICKLY ('CUZ GUESTS ARE COMING OVER!)

1. Take out the trash.

2. Clean the mirrors and windows.
3. Get dirty dishes out of the sink.
4. Make your bed.
5. Do something with that pile of paper.
6. Vacuum the common areas.
7. Do a quick wipe-down of the bathroom.
8. Light a candle.

JUST A REMINDER FOR THOSE OF YOU WITH CHILDREN . . .

Your children are not the center of the home.

My children are a blessing.

Most of the time.

It has certainly been work raising them, and there have been moments along the way when I wondered how I would get through certain parenting phases . . . or if my kids would survive them! The miracle of it all is looking at their faces and seeing some of me, some of Philip, and mostly just them. They are wonderfully unique individuals with their own purposes in God.

For many of us, children are part of our lives as we work out our marriages. We might want to ship them off to Siberia sometimes, but we don't . . . although I now know people who live there, so if you are interested, we have connections! ☻ Of course, we invest tremendous amounts of time, energy and affection in our kids—and that's a good thing. The problem is when our children become the center of our marriage.

From birth to 18 years old is 6,570 days (well, it is if you don't count leap years). This is roughly the amount of time your children will be with you on a daily basis. Obviously, our children remain our children forever, but the daily input will last for about 6,570 days. If Philip and I are blessed to have a 60-year marriage (just 33 more years to go!), we will have been married for 21,900 days.

6,570 days.

21,900 days.

Do the math.

Assuming all goes as we hope it will, the time our children spend living with us is much shorter than the span of our marriage, which is why it is not in the best interest of the relationship to make our children the center of it. They are a vital part, but not the center.

I made this mistake with my son, Jordan. After he was born, I did not leave him—even for a few hours—for many months. He was the center of my world. His needs took priority over Philip's. His cry was louder and more demanding, so I accommodated him. What ended up happening was that my marriage wound up on the back burner. This certainly wasn't a conscious decision—it just happened as I looked to meet my child's needs instead of my husband's. Eventually I started feeling more and more disconnected from Philip.

I had some ground to make up.

Fixing the problem was as simple as realizing a few things. First, I needed to get Jordan on some kind of schedule, so that he fit in with our family instead of running it. There are some great parenting resources out there that can help with this. It is so important! Your children are a blessing from God . . . not to distract you from His purpose, but to join you on the journey.

Secondly, I realized that I needed to go on a date with my husband. We needed to spend some hours together as a couple. Jordan would be fine.

Over the years, we have learned that regardless of the ages of our children, we need time as a couple. Time away from the kids. Time to remind each other that we got together for relationship, and not just the work of a marriage. Often, if we don't take that time, our communication can simply be:

"Who's cooking dinner?"

"Who's picking up the kids?"

"Did you sign the permission slip?"

"He forgot his lunch—can you take it to the school?"

This is all necessary communication, but intimacy requires just a bit more!

Do your homework to find a good babysitter, and then go out to dinner or go on a walk. It doesn't really matter what the activity is—just that it's something where you reconnect on a regular basis.

We have also made it a practice to have not only family vacations, but also Philip and Holly vacations. When our children were younger, we might just be gone for a few nights, and then come back and get the kids before embarking on our longer family vacation. But eventually, it got to be that Philip and I would spend a week together somewhere . . . just the two of us. Then Paris and Jordan might join us. But that week alone with Philip would remind me why I married him! We needed that time away as a couple.

I have talked to some couples with young children who say they would love to go out, but their children cry when they leave . . . and that makes it too hard. I understand that. I remember how difficult it was initially to leave our children in the hands of a babysitter, no matter how qualified the sitter was. But let me tell you what going out on a date teaches the children. It teaches them that the husband-wife relationship is a very high priority in the family. It teaches them that Mommy and Daddy love to spend time together. The best thing you and your spouse can do for your children is to love each other.

We are to love our kids. We want the best for them. But making them the center of the family universe is not in their best interests. Nor does it serve our world to have a generation of young people who think the world revolves around them. It will certainly not serve your marriage well either.

I also found we had to be careful about how many activities Jordan and Paris got involved in. I have loved watching them both play various sports over the years. But I have tried to limit it to one at a time. Otherwise, Philip and I would be so busy keeping up with their schedules that it would be tricky for us, in our already very full lives, to find time together.

Another thing to remember is that it's important for parents to present a united front. Do not let your children, or their desires, drive a wedge between you and your spouse. If you disagree about the way something should be handled with the kids . . . driving, curfew, spending the night away from home, whatever . . . don't disagree in front of them. Go discuss the issue behind closed doors, and then present whatever decision you come to together to your children.

Really, parenting is the process of teaching and training your children to leave your home and begin lives of their own. That might sound strange, but it is true. Our job is to equip our kids to leave us well.

(Just as a confession . . . I am already working on my apology to the woman who marries my son. I failed. While he is one of the smartest, most compassionate and fun-loving young men I know [that's the part I did right!], he has no idea how to do laundry or clean anything. Maybe there is some sort of crash course I can send him to!)

> Therefore a man shall leave his father and mother and be joined to his wife, and they shall become one flesh (Gen. 2:24, NKJV).

Children are supposed to leave, and parents are supposed to stay. Thus the marriage should be at the top of the chart. Navigating life with children is fun, but it is also hard work. Don't let the work of it cause you to lose sight of each other.

TEN THOUGHTS ABOUT PREGNANCY

1. **Pray!** There is nothing more important than praying for your new baby, your relationship with your spouse, and the transition into parenting. God is the creator of life and the One who will give you peace and comfort in this exciting and challenging season. Pray, pray, pray!

2. **Stay healthy.** Contrary to popular belief, pregnancy is not a free pass to eat whatever you want! Sure, there are times to indulge in a bowl of ice cream in the name of cravings, but you will have a better pregnancy, labor, delivery and recovery if you stay healthy. Remember that the things you are eating and drinking are going straight to your developing baby; make healthy choices most of the time, and save the indulging for special occasions. (Speaking of which, did you know that any calories consumed at your own baby shower don't count!?) Start your day with a healthy breakfast, always carry a water bottle, and keep lots of healthy snacks in your purse, car and desk—this will help you make good choices

throughout the day. Continue to exercise (talk to your doctor if you are unsure about what you should and shouldn't do).

3. **Get connected with other moms.** We are not meant to do life alone, especially when raising children! Find other moms with whom you can connect, share advice (and clothes!), swap tips, and pray. Join a new moms' group so you can share the season you're in together. It's equally important to find moms with older kids to get a different perspective. If you don't know those moms, look for older kids whom you would love to see your baby emulate one day—take those kids' moms to lunch and ask lots of questions!

4. **It's not all about the baby.** It may seem like your whole world is focused on your baby right now, but make an effort not to completely succumb to babymania. I'm sure your friends who don't have kids are very excited for you, but they probably don't want to hear every detail of your latest OB appointment. Just sayin'. Plus, your pregnancy is a great time to focus on your dreams and passions as a mother and as a daughter of the King. Fulfilling your own purpose will help your kids discover theirs. You may need to make a few changes in your life in those first years of parenthood, but don't lose sight

of your God-given purpose in the midst of diapers and midnight feedings. Stay connected beyond your baby—keep serving at church, read books that have more than five words on a page, go out on a date with your husband, or have a baby-free girls night. Ask someone to keep you accountable on this one, because it's very easy to get caught in the baby bubble!

5. **Educate yourself.** Unfortunately, babies don't come with manuals! It is up to you to educate yourself about your pregnancy, delivery and parenting options. Read, learn and ask questions. Even if all your friends did something one way, do your own research and decide what is best for your family. There is a lot of good (and bad!) information out there, so be sure to look at a lot of different resources—no one is responsible for your pregnancy and baby except for you (and your husband).

6. **Trust your instincts.** God has given you everything you need to be an excellent mother. Isn't that amazing?? Go to Him every day (see #1) and ask Him to give you the peace, patience and understanding to make great decisions for your child. When something just doesn't seem right, trust that the Holy Spirit is the primary source of your capabilities as a mother—stop and listen.

7. **Assemble a good team around you.** Thankfully, there are many resources available to you during pregnancy, delivery, recovery and parenting. Choose your support team carefully—doctors, midwives, doulas, nurses, lactation consultants, birth educators, pediatricians and whomever else you wish to involve. Make sure you feel comfortable with the people who will be helping you bring this new life into the world. You will be so happy to have a team you trust during this very emotional and precious time of life.

8. **Include your spouse.** Let's be honest, there are a lot of elements of pregnancy and new babies that just freak some men out. You may have a husband who wants to make every decision with you, or one who is completely confused and overwhelmed by the whole thing. Make sure you are including him and valuing his opinion. It might seem easier to make decisions on your own or with your mom, sister or girlfriend. But if you shut out your husband now, don't expect him to jump into Super Dad mode overnight. Establish yourself and your husband as a parenting team early on, and make sure he knows how valuable he is.

9. **Be thankful.** Come from a place of gratitude, thanking God every day for the blessing of being able to carry His creation. This attitude will change your pregnancy. Women who live in a place of thankfulness

have healthier pregnancies and a better transition into motherhood. Of course, there are moments (morning sickness, anyone!?) that are not comfortable or fun, but complaining constantly won't help and can be hurtful to the many women who are not able to get pregnant. Focus on the prize at the end of your discomfort—a sweet baby!

10. **Don't compare.** This is your pregnancy, not a competition. It's so easy to compare weight gain, baby development, parenting choices, nursery decor, and a hundred other things. Allow yourself to enjoy your pregnancy journey for what it is for you, not what it is compared to your friend's pregnancy. Don't waste your time on jealousy or competition; be confident in who God created you to be and you will enjoy your pregnancy so much more!

SEVEN WAYS TO COMMUNICATE WITH YOUR CHILD

According to author Deanne C. Haisch, M.A., if getting your child to do something feels like an impossible task, it may be because of the way you are asking. The instructions we give to our children must be spoken in a way that they will understand. Here are some helpful hints on how to give your kids instructions that will make both you and your child more successful.

1. **Get your child's attention.** Make sure you have your child's attention before you give a direction. Doing this will help your son or daughter know that you are speaking to him or her. Call your child's name, make eye contact, or turn off the light. Also, try to put yourself within about three feet of your child so you can speak at a normal volume and in a calm voice.

2. **Be clear and concise.** Make sure your instructions are short and to the point. A good guide is one word per year of life (for example, instruction for a two-year-old might be "shoes on," while you could tell a five-year-old to "go get your shoes on"). If you use too many words, your children will have difficulty in knowing what is expected of them. The instruction should also be free of vague words.

3. **Give one instruction at a time.** Giving multiple instructions to your child can overwhelm him or her.

4. **Be realistic.** Give your child instructions that you know he or she can actually follow.

5. **Be positive.** Tell your child what you want him or her to *do* rather than *not do*. If you only describe a negative behavior ("don't run"), you leave the door open for your child to some other types of behaviors that you don't want (skipping, hopping, sliding). However, if

you give a positive direction ("please walk"), it closes the door on your child doing other options.

6. **Don't ask, tell.** Always try to tell your child in a firm but pleasant voice what you want him or her to do. Again, don't say something like, "Will you not run in the hallway?" as this might indicate to your child that he or she has a choice in the matter. Instead, say, "Please walk in the hallway."

7. **Reward compliance.** Let your child know when he or she does a good job following your instructions. The more you praise your child, the better the chances are that he or she will follow your directions in the future.[1]

TEN INEXPENSIVE WAYS TO ENTERTAIN YOUNG CHILDREN

1. Bubbles!

2. Play in the dirt with spoons and bowls.

3. Large cardboard boxes.

4. Paper airplanes.

5. Hopscotch.
6. Turn on the music and dance!
7. Homemade pizza (they get to put whatever they want on theirs!)
8. Water sprinkler.
9. Make a tin-can telephone.
10. Go read books at the library.

GET PLANTED!!!

The righteous will flourish like a palm tree, they will grow like a cedar of Lebanon; ***planted in the house of the Lord, they will flourish in the courts of our God.*** *They will still bear fruit in old age, they will stay fresh and green.*

PSALM 92:12-14 (EMPHASIS ADDED)

The Bible is pretty clear. If we want our lives to flourish—and I would imagine most of us do—we must be planted in the house of God . . . in church. Planted. Not just attending. But planted, with roots going down, taking in nutrients, and leaves sprouting, giving off oxygen.

Planted. Learning, growing and serving.

Planted. Not moving from church to church.

Planted. So that people know you.

Planted. So that people can hold you accountable to living the God-life.

Planted. So that when life is hard, people know how to pray for you.

Planted. So that when life is good, people celebrate with you.

Interestingly enough, the Bible does not say we will flourish if we have a great job, buy a great house, or live in a great neighborhood. No. It says our life will flourish if we are planted in the house of God. All of the good stuff—including a strong marriage and healthy family—comes out of being planted in God's house.

My life revolves around being planted in the house of God. I don't just clock in and out, as if my attending church is an obligation or is doing God a big favor. No. I am committed to these people in my world. We are not just "church friends." We call it "doing life together." We are every day, every season kind of friends.

The theme song of the old sitcom *Cheers* basically says that we all want to go to places where we are known and where people are glad to see us. That's what happens when you are planted in God's house. You are known and valued.

Maybe you are experiencing such pain in a relationship right now that loneliness is overwhelming you. You and I were created for relationship, so when there is a disconnect, we feel lonely and isolated. I have good news:

> God sets the lonely in families (Ps. 68:6).

He brings the lonely, which is often you and me, into the family and house of God . . . to connect and to do life with people!

Connecting into a life-giving church is one of the best things you can do for yourself and your marriage.

Because I am planted in God's house, I have surrounded myself with people who are committed to making a difference on the planet. We are determined to build healthy homes because we realize that as our own homes and families get stronger, we become better equipped to minister to others in our world.

And that's why we are here! To bring light into dark places. Our churches and our families should be beacons of light, guiding those who are frustrated, hurt, lost and confused to the place where they can receive help and refreshing. Sometimes one of the best things you can do is take your eyes off your own pain for a moment and focus on helping other hurting people.

MORE, PLEASE!

(Additional Reading)

Clueless: 10 Things I Wish I Knew About Motherhood Before Becoming a Mom by Kerri Weems

Making Children Mind without Losing Yours by Dr. Kevin Leman

Organizing from the Inside Out by Julie Morgenstern

9

Moving Forward

OVERCOMING HURTS OF THE PAST

You are responsible for your life. You can't keep blaming somebody else for your dysfunction. Life is really about moving on.

OPRAH WINFREY

EXCESS BAGGAGE

Excess baggage. It's expensive. It's heavy. It tends to get in the way of perfectly good legroom or hog all the space in an overhead compartment. No one particularly likes it . . . mostly because it slows everyone down.

Then there's the excess baggage of the heart: those less-than-perfect experiences of the past that have a way of weighing us down on our way to the future . . .

Betrayals . . . Insecurities . . . Rejections . . . Failures . . . Heartbreak . . . Fear . . . Abuse . . . Addictions . . . Shame . . .

A word was spoken in anger. A parent was too busy working to notice a need. A father abandoned the home. A friend betrayed our trust. A boyfriend unexpectedly ended the relationship. A business deal didn't go as planned. A few bad decisions left us wallowing in guilt and shame.

It doesn't matter whether we were raised in a strong Christian home with loving parents or in a harmful, dysfunctional home (or, like many of us, somewhere in between). Regardless of our experience, one thing is certain: We each have our own excess baggage of the heart. And what we do with it matters.

Quite honestly, this type of baggage is far more dangerous and costly than a couple of extra carry-ons at the airport. Overweight luggage may slow us down just enough to miss a connecting flight, but untended wounds of the heart have the potential to slow us down just enough to miss out on our God-given destiny.

I (Nicole) had more than my share of excess baggage as a 19-year-old first stepping through the doors of what has since become my church home (Oasis Church).

You see, I grew up in a home with two funny, smart and hard-working parents who frequently told me they loved me . . .

. . . They just didn't always show it in the best possible way. They had some excess baggage from their own childhood experiences, and all that baggage left them unable to create the healthiest environment for my older sister and me.

My father was an alcoholic until I was 10 years old. This caused constant tension, which often erupted in the form of my parents fighting and threatening each other with divorce. My father, feeling disrespected in his own home, would regularly lash out at my mom. Though I couldn't articulate it at the time, I now realize that my mother was both verbally and emotionally abused by my father on a regular basis.

These of course were things we never discussed outside of our home. Even within the family, we struggled to give voice to our feelings. My sister and I often found ourselves (from a very early age) looking after the emotional well-being of both of our parents. In many ways, this left us confused about what healthy and loving relationships looked like.

By the time I reached my late teens, I had discovered my voice in my home—it was loud and it was angry! Years of bitterness and resentment toward my father came out in a number of full-on, hold-nothing-back fights. We really duked it out! In the end, neither of us emerged the victor of those emotional boxing matches. We both lost. We lost our relationship.

For about two years, we lived under the same roof, but hardly spoke a word to each other. Our conversations began and ended with one of us saying, "Pass the salt" at the dinner table.

I never realized until then just how painful silence could be.

When I left home and moved to Los Angeles to pursue an acting career, I couldn't get away fast enough. I wanted nothing to do with my father. The more distance I could put between myself and my family, the better!

I had surrendered my life to Jesus when I was 12 years old. I accepted His salvation and pursued His plans for my life.

None of that changed the fact that I was an emotional mess when I first became a part of my local church 10 years ago. I was broken by the wounds of my childhood, and I was relationally isolated and afraid. I didn't know how to connect with people. I didn't even know how to identify people who were safe to connect with. I was extremely guarded and preferred to find love in how well I performed than in healthy, Christian friendships and relationships.

Talk about baggage!

I'm so thankful for the healing journey God has taken me on as a young woman! He has been faithful to heal my wounds and bring joy and strength to my relationships! God has also done MIRACLES (some suddenly, but most of them years in the making) in my family! My father overcame his addiction to alcohol. My parents have done the hard work of saving their marriage and are happily married to this day! I now have a loving and healthy relationship with my father!

God has taught me how to let go of my past and my hurts, and He can do the same for you! Jesus gave His life for us so that we might become healthy and whole. God doesn't want any of us to live our lives hurting and alone. You and I were fashioned and created for so much more!

My prayer is that as you read this chapter, you will have the courage to hand over your excess baggage to Jesus and learn how to pursue a whole and healthy heart! The truth is that you and I weren't meant to carry excess baggage, and Jesus is the only One strong enough *to* carry it. You may have to unpack some of those nicely kept but unbearably heavy issues of the soul—and that can be painful—but I am confident that as you open the hurting places of your heart to Him, you will begin to experience what it means to live light and free!

> Come to me, all you who are weary and burdened, and I will give you rest. Take my yoke upon you and learn from me, for I am gentle and humble in heart, and you will find rest for your souls. For my yoke is easy and my burden is light (Matt. 11:28-30).

WHO'S SAFE?

When I (Nicole) was four years old, my family moved to 8th Street, where we lived in a beige house at the end of a cul-de-sac. That house became more than a house; for the next 10 years, it was home. Similarly, 8th Street became more than a residential street; it served as the setting for my many adventures with my two neighborhood friends, Rick and Brandon.

It was my mom who first encouraged me to go introduce myself to Rick and Brandon. She saw me watching them through my bedroom window as they played outside. They were playing catch, and I desperately wanted to join them.

For two days, I continued to watch them. That's how long it took me to work up the courage to leave my safe bedroom viewpoint and awkwardly ask if I could play with them.

I hated being the new kid in the neighborhood.

I was afraid they would laugh at me and tell me I couldn't play with them because I was a girl. To my surprise, we exchanged names, and by the end of the week we were all best friends.

For the next eight years, we were inseparable. We dreamed dreams together, laughed together, and occasionally fought with one another. We always had each other's backs, and we each believed we were the best friends anyone could ever ask for.

I'll admit we occasionally even got into a little mischief together. ☻

Our parents used to call us the Three Musketeers. We were too little to really understand the reference, but we understood that it meant something special . . .

We understood that our friendship was something special.

We each eventually moved away from our childhood neighborhood, and our adventures together came to an end. In fact, it's been 16 years since we've seen one another.

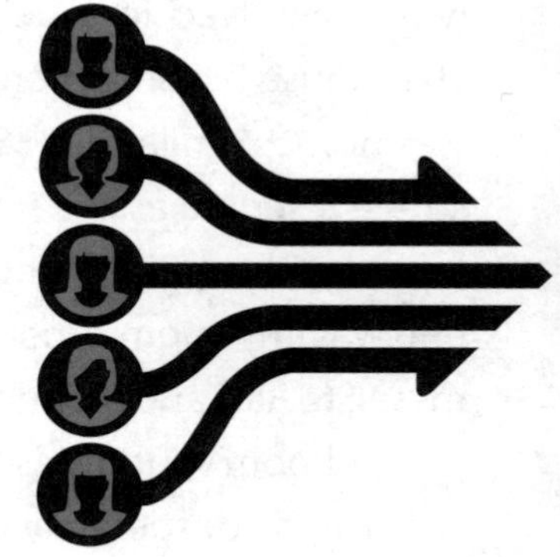

But I will be forever grateful for Rick and Brandon and the childhood memories we shared.

As I've gotten older, I've realized that friendships and relationships don't come that easily. It takes more than a week of playing catch on 8th Street to become best friends. We have to work a bit harder to create truly special relationships. A key part of the process is figuring out which people are safe to develop relationships with.

It can be hard to recognize who the safe people are, especially if, like me, you were not always exposed to safe people in your home growing up. But healthy, Jesus-centered relationships are ones where both you and the other person are **safe.** Below are two lists to help guide you. While reading over these lists, you may want to think and pray about how you can become a safer person and ask yourself how you can actively choose to invest in relationships with safe people.

TEN QUALITIES OF SAFE PEOPLE

1. Safe people have authentic, growing relationships with Jesus and are pursuing His plans for their lives.
2. They are able to engage in healthy conflict, speaking truth in love and working through differences.
3. They are accepting of others and show grace to those around them.
4. They have great relationships with other friends besides you and encourage you to have great relationships with other friends besides them.
5. They have values similar to yours.

6. They are quick to forgive.

7. They avoid gossip and bad-mouthing others.

8. They are eager to serve and help others.

9. They are generous with their time and resources.

10. They want to learn and grow in all areas of life.

TEN QUALITIES OF UNSAFE PEOPLE

1. Unsafe people have a hard time admitting when they are struggling with something or going through a tough time.

2. They are defensive and receive advice as criticism.

3. They are overly critical of others.

4. They consistently fail to follow through with what they said they would do.

5. They blame others instead of taking responsibility for their own actions.

6. They are envious of others' successes and frequently compare themselves to others.

7. They get jealous of other friendships you are investing in.

8. They lie to avoid consequences and conflict.

9. They have a hard time respecting and honoring those in positions of authority.

10. They try to influence and encourage you to do things that will negatively impact your relationship with Jesus.

THE F-WORD: FORGIVENESS

Without forgiveness, there's no future.

ARCHBISHOP DESMOND TUTU

Archbishop Tutu knows what he's talking about. The only way to move forward and embrace the grand purpose and destiny God has in store for each of us is to forgive those who have wronged us in the past.

Now I know that for many of us, this concept of forgiveness is a hard pill to swallow. In fact, some of you reading this may be contemplating stapling this section of the book together and never looking at it again!

Many of you are thinking . . .

"Well, you don't know what he did to me."

"You've never had those harsh words spoken to you."

"What they did is just too cruel to forgive."

You are right. I don't know what you've been through . . . and I am deeply sorry that you have been wounded and hurt by those you've trusted. Something I do know is that our heavenly Father is head over heels in love with you, and He is not for a minute okay with the wrongs that have been done to you!

I also know that what's even worse than the pain of our pasts is what happens to us when we allow that pain to plague our presents and sabotage our futures.

Unforgiveness is a trap. It keeps us chained to pain and disappointment, and unable to freely embrace the abundant life that Jesus came, died and rose from the dead to give us.

Unforgiveness is also like a cancer that spreads in our souls. It taints all of our relationships, ambitions and experiences with bitterness and resentment. It's the worst kind of disease, with the capacity to destroy any of our hopes for the future.

I (Nicole) will never forget hearing a woman share her story at a GodChicks night many years ago. I was 19 years old and fiercely loyal to the idea of never forgiving my father for what I had experienced in my home growing up. I was completely bitter and angry and determined to keep as much distance as possible between my father and me. Of course, these are the sorts of thoughts I didn't articulate to my Christian friends. In fact, I made it a point not to talk about my feelings toward my dad with anyone, mostly because I knew how ugly and unkind these feelings really were.

Instead, I had made a choice in my heart not to speak to my father. For a little while, I kept that resolution.

But that all changed as I sat listening to this courageous woman share the story of abuse she had been exposed to in her home as a child. She shared about how a real relationship with Jesus had brought healing and hope to her life. She described this healing journey as a process, and said an important step in that process was FORGIVENESS. She recognized that she had to forgive her mother and father for what had been done to her when she was a child. She encouraged all of us to make the strong, hard choice to forgive those who had wronged us.

I thought, *Forgiveness?! You've got to be kidding me! I am never going to forgive my dad! He should be asking me for forgiveness, and until he does, I'm not even going to entertain the thought!*

But no matter how hard I tried to fight it, by the time she reached the end of her story, I knew that as much as I hated the idea of forgiveness, it was what God was leading me to do . . .

I kicked and screamed in my heart over the idea. I cried and prayed all the way home that night. I remember praying, "This is too hard, God. I can't do it. How am I supposed to forgive him? Why would You ask me to do something this hard? Don't You love me?"

I truly believe this was our loving and wonderful heavenly Father's response to me: "I do love you. More than you could ever know. It's because I love you that I want you to forgive. I want you free, and you won't be free without forgiveness."

That night I called my father. We hadn't exchanged words in a very long time. In fact, I was surprised that he took my call. I suppose he was just as surprised that I had called in the first place.

I clenched the phone in my hand so tightly that my knuckles turned white. My hands wouldn't stop shaking. I struggled to control my voice as it cracked and swayed under the weight of confined tears.

To my dismay, and by God's grace, I listened as these words poured out of my mouth: "Papi, I just wanted to call to tell you that I love you. And I am sorry. I want to ask for your forgiveness, because for so long I have been angry and bitter toward you. That's not right of me. I want you to know that I love you, and I am deeply sorry my love has been in question."

Then came an awkward silence that seemed to last forever. It may have been the longest pause of my life.

My father finally spoke. I could hear the tears in his shaking voice as he told me that he loved me, and that it was he who was sorry for all that had taken place.

It wasn't a long conversation that night. But some things don't have to be everlasting to be eternal.

My relationship with my father wasn't supernaturally repaired in one night. It had taken years for the brokenness to be formed, and it would take years for it to fully mend. But a bridge of reconciliation that I never imagined possible was built over the act of FORGIVENESS.

Perhaps even more miraculous was the shift that had taken place in my heart. It was as if a chain wrapped around me had burst open. I was beginning to understand the personal freedom that comes with forgiveness. Once I experienced this type of freedom, I resolved never to willingly allow myself to be chained and weighted down by unforgiveness again.

Forgiveness unlocks purpose and destiny. It allows us to run freely toward our future. It replaces skepticism with hope, and bitterness with love. Forgiveness is not an emotion. If you stop and think about it, you'll realize that forgiveness is never anything we naturally feel like doing.

No, forgiveness is a choice. It's a choice we have to make over and over again. We may have to choose in our hearts to forgive someone a hundred times before the pain of the wrong loses its sting.

In fact, Jesus addressed this very point with His disciples:

> Then Peter came to him and asked, "Lord, how often should I forgive someone who sins against me? Seven times?"
>
> "No, not seven times," Jesus replied, "but seventy times seven!" (Matt. 18:21-22, NLT).

It is worth noting that forgiveness is not an invitation to allow someone to continue to harm us. I am so thankful that I was able to reconcile with my father and rebuild a loving relationship with him. For some of us, that may not be an option. There is a difference between forgiving someone and putting yourself in a harmful situation. You may need to seek the advice and support of your pastor or another Christian leader to help you navigate a particular situation. Remember, forgiveness is something we freely give, but trust is something that is earned.

Whether or not relationships are made new, our perspective on life certainly is. Forgiveness unleashes the God-given potential for greatness that lies within each of us. My prayer is that you will have the courage to embrace the type of freedom only accessible through FORGIVENESS. After all, you were made for far more than a life confined by past hurts.

DIRTY MINDS

Usually this phrase is associated with crude jokes, and it is often followed by someone adding, "Get your head out of the gutter!"

Though impure thoughts are certainly one element of a less-than-squeaky-clean mind, there are all kinds of thoughts that pollute our brains as they run through them!

"I'm not pretty enough."

"I'm not smart enough."

"I'm a loser."

"If people knew the real me, they would reject me."

"God is angry at me."

"I'm going to end up all alone."

"Something bad is going to happen—I just know it."

This is not the way God thinks about us. He loves us, and His thoughts toward us are good and loving!

A key to overcoming our past hurts is to recognize these types of filthy thoughts and throw them in the trash! Then, to make sure these thoughts stay in the dumpster where they belong, we must discover and focus on what God thinks about us!

We purify our minds when we get rid of negative thoughts and replace them with God-thoughts!

The great news is that we don't have to wonder what God thinks about us! He makes His thoughts clear and accessible to us through His Word. So grab your Bible, read, and let God's Word perform a deep cleaning of your mind!

WHAT GOD REALLY THINKS ABOUT YOU . . .

. . . YOU are the loved-beyond-measure daughter of the King.

God put his love on the line for us by offering his Son in sacrificial death while we were of no use whatever to him (Rom. 5:8, THE MESSAGE).

My choice is you, God, first and only.
And now I find I'm your choice!
You set me up with a house and yard.
And then you made me your heir!
(Ps. 16:5-6, THE MESSAGE).

. . . YOU are precious and valuable to God.

Are not five sparrows sold for two pennies? And [yet] not one of them is forgotten or uncared for in the presence of God. But [even] the very hairs of your head are all numbered. Do not be struck with fear or seized with alarm; you are of greater worth than many [flocks] of sparrows (Luke 12:6-7, AMP).

. . . YOU are beautiful in the sight of God.

Gabriel greeted her:
Good morning!
You're beautiful with God's beauty,
Beautiful inside and out!
God be with you (Luke 1:28, THE MESSAGE).

. . . YOU are wonderfully made.

When I look at the night sky
and see the work of your fingers—
The moon and the stars you set in place
What are mere mortals
that you should think about them,
Human beings that you should care for them?
Yet you made them only a little lower than God
and crowned them with glory and honor (Ps. 8:3-5, NLT).

. . . YOU are never alone; God is always with you.

He [God] Himself has said, I will not in any way fail you nor give you up nor leave you without support. [I will] not, [I will] not, [I will] not in any degree leave you helpless nor forsake nor let [you] down (relax My hold on you)! [Assuredly not!] (Heb. 13:5, AMP).

. . . YOU are not defined by your past, but you are now a new creation in Christ Jesus.

Therefore if any person is [ingrafted] in Christ (the Messiah) he is a new creation (a new creature altogether); the old [previous moral and spiritual condition] has passed away. Behold, the fresh and new has come! (2 Cor. 5:17, AMP).

. . . YOU have a hope and a future in Jesus.

For I know the thoughts and plans that I have for you, says the Lord, thoughts and plans for welfare and peace and not for evil, to give you hope in your final outcome (Jer. 29:11, AMP).

. . . YOU have a special purpose and destiny.

We are assured and know that [God being a partner in their labor] all things work together and are [fitting into a plan] for good to and for those who love God and are called according to [His] design and purpose (Rom. 8:28, AMP).

. . . YOU can do all things through Jesus who gives you strength.

I know how to be abased, and I know how to abound. Everywhere and in all things I have learned both to be full and to be hungry, both to abound and to suffer need. I can do all things through Christ who strengthens me (Phil. 4:12-13, NKJV).

SUIT UP!

Overcoming past hurts is no small task! In fact, it's a battle of the mind—perhaps the greatest battle you will ever face.

A soldier goes to battle suited up for a fight! You won't find her engaging the enemy in a summer dress and some flip-flops! She enters the war zone with a helmet, a bulletproof vest, camouflage, boots, and a deadly weapon.

When it comes to overcoming our pasts, we too need to dress the part! The Bible describes this very outfit in Ephesians 6:13-17:

> Therefore, put on every piece of God's armor so you will be able to resist the enemy in the time of evil. Then after the battle you will still be standing firm. Stand your ground, putting on the belt of truth and the body armor of God's righteousness. For shoes, put on the peace that comes from the Good News so that you will be fully prepared. In addition to all of these, hold up the shield of faith to stop the fiery arrows of the devil. Put on salvation as your helmet, and take the sword of the Spirit, which is the word of God (NLT).

Determine to overcome the wounds of your past! Stand your ground! Take back what the enemy of your soul has stolen! Defeat every insecurity, fear, doubt and worry you are attacked with! Your victory begins the moment you decide to suit up!

THE PERFECT SMILE

She dresses with strength and nobility, and she smiles at the future.

PROVERBS 31:25, GOD'S WORD

Life is made up of moments—so many, in fact, that we would never be able to remember them all. Some memories seem a bit random, while some memories we wish we could forget. Others we simply treasure . . .

The moment we held that diploma in our hand. The moment we first saw our groom as we walked down the aisle. The moment our boss told us all our hard work didn't go unnoticed, and we got the promotion. The moment we said yes to the nervous but adorable guy who just asked us to coffee. The moment the doctor confirmed we were pregnant.

These are the types of moments that have a way of leaving big smiles on our faces. In fact, some of us are grinning ear-to-ear just thinking about them!

The same way we smile at these special moments in our pasts, God wants us to smile at our futures. He doesn't want us to be afraid of what might happen—or worried about how it will all turn out. If you are like me, then perhaps some experiences from your past have left you skeptical of your future. You may believe that something bad always ends up happening. Maybe you are convinced that people close to you will end up hurting you, rejecting you, or abandoning you.

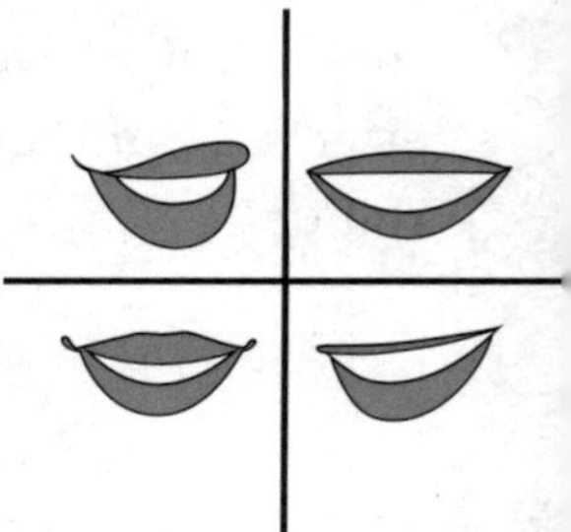

When we entrust our lives to Jesus, we discover that His plans for us are good! We can walk confidently into the future, because we know that He is with us, leading and guiding us each step of the way! We don't have to live in fear that our pasts will rewrite themselves in our futures. God has His very best in store for us! That's not to say there won't be any more challenging moments. There will be. That's an inevitability we can't avoid. But when we follow Jesus, we can live in the certainty that we can overcome any and every challenge that comes our way! And we can always anticipate that when it comes to following Jesus, the best is yet to come!

Are you able to smile at your future? Do you trust that Jesus has His very best in store for you as you daily follow Him? What fears and doubts from your past are stealing your joy about the future?

Choose today—and every day—to trust Jesus with what's to come! Go ahead and show off those pearly whites! ☻ Your best days lie ahead!

LOOK AROUND

When it comes to our own hurts, it's easy to develop a bit of tunnel vision. The emotional aftermath of a painful experience can feel all-consuming. If we're not careful, our own pain can blind us to the needs of those around us.

God not only wants us to notice the needs of others, but He also positions us to lend a helping hand. When you and I reach beyond our own pain to lift someone else up, we discover strength we didn't know we had! As crazy as it may seem, God uses our simplest acts of service to bring healing and purpose to our hearts.

Here are a few ideas for serving others as you embark on healing the wounds of your past:

1. Begin serving in your local church and discover how you can use your unique gifts and talents in God's house!

2. Share your story with someone who is struggling in an area you have overcome. By sharing what Jesus has done in your life and what you have learned, you can be the encouragement someone else desperately needs!

3. Volunteer at a homeless shelter or other nonprofit organization with which your local church partners.

4. Be a "big sister" to a younger woman in your world, cheering her on and giving her advice as she navigates seasons of life you have already walked through.

5. Take the time this week to ask a friend, family member or coworker how they are really doing. Listen and see if there is any way you can be of help or support to them.

CALL FOR BACKUP

I (Nicole) love cop shows. I used to watch them religiously with my dad. I would then reenact my favorite scenes with my next-door neighbors, Rick and Brandon.

Brandon always insisted on being the detective. (Everyone wanted to be the detective because, well, he was the hero, but we let Brandon have his way because it was the only way we could get him to play.)

Rick was always the bad guy.

I rotated parts depending on what the script called for. Sometimes I was the hostage. Sometimes I was an accomplice.

But my absolute favorite was when I got to play Detective Brandon's backup.

He would call on me when things got crazy—when shots were being fired, and everyone was dodging bullets. He would call in for backup . . . which when you're nine years old, basically means yelling the phrase "backup!" in between making fake gunshot noises and imagining bullets flying out of your gun-pointed-hands.

I loved being my friend's backup. It meant I got to be part of the action. I helped save the day. Together, we caught the bad guy and made the world a safer place.

It's been close to 20 years since I played a game of "cops and robbers," but that doesn't mean I haven't been called in for backup over the years.

Providing backup and calling for backup are parts of developing a healthy life. When we lose jobs or have marital problems or struggle to know whether or not to end dating relationships or try to lose weight and get in shape, we need friends and mentors to be our backup—people who can encourage and inspire us in our faith.

When a friend or family member is navigating a divorce or overcoming an addiction or working on the ability to communicate respectfully or dealing with the loss of a loved one, we get to be backup for them, ready to support them the best way we can.

The truth is that we need each other. We will never overcome the hurts of our pasts on our own. We were created to do life together. Sometimes that means being willing to call for backup . . .

Together we can catch the culprit who seeks to destroy our souls, and we will make our world a much better place!

FIVE WAYS TO SILENCE CRITICISM

The apostle Paul certainly experienced his share of criticism.

Most leaders do.

The person out front is always the easiest to criticize. Paul had a way of dealing with criticism that he passed along to his protégé Timothy:

> Don't let anyone look down on you because you are young, but set an example for the believers in speech, in life, in love, in faith and in purity (1 Tim. 4:12, TNIV).

One of the difficulties Timothy had to overcome was his youth. The word translated "young" or "youth" is the Greek word *neotes*, which can describe anyone of military age, up to age 40. The Church usually liked its leaders to be people of maturity. Timothy was certainly younger than Paul, and many would watch him with a critical eye. Paul explained to Timothy that the only way to silence criticism was through his conduct. This is hard advice to follow . . . and yet, it's the only possible way.

Timothy was challenged to be an example—and so are we. Fighting with our critics never accomplishes much, so let's just commit ourselves to living exemplary lives. In what ways?

In speech. Words are powerful. The apostle James tells us that in many ways, our words set the course of our lives (see Jas. 3:3-8). What kind of speech is coming out of your mouth? In the heat of the moment, what words are you uttering? Do they honor God? Are they building faith in the hearers? Are they kind? Defensive? Arrogant? Do you feel the need to have the last word? Are you talking too much?

In conduct. How are you behaving? Would you want someone imitating your behavior? Are you leading a disciplined life? Or is there an area that is a bit out of control? Are you kind? Hospitable? Gracious? Forgiving? Do you demand your own way? Are you willing to take second place? Or do you need to be in front? Are you serving anyone or anywhere? WWJD . . . really?

In love. This word is *agape*. One of the definitions is "unconquerable benevolence." If we have *agape*, then no matter what anyone does to us or says about us, we will seek nothing but their good. Ordinarily love comes from the heart, but this kind of love comes from the will. This is the kind of love that refuses to get bitter, never hates, always forgives, and cares for others no matter what they have done. This kind of love, according to Bible scholar

William Barclay, will take the whole of our nature and strength of character to achieve. To silence our critics, we will need to love like this. How are you doing in this department?

In faith. This word in the Greek is *pistis* and implies an absolute conviction that God is Creator and Jesus is Messiah. This word also means loyalty—a loyalty that defies circumstances. Do you trust God when things aren't going the way you planned? Can you remain loyal in the middle of the battle? Are you really trusting God with your life? Your money? Your relationships?

In purity. As Christians, we have committed ourselves to lives of purity. Regardless of how bad our pasts may have been, once we begin to walk with Jesus, we are committing to a different way of life. Our sins have been washed away, and we are as white as snow. Now we have to walk that out. We won't do it perfectly—we will mess up from time to time and need to ask for forgiveness—however we must turn from our old ways and pursue His way. We have to have a different standard of behavior, of self-control and discipline. Pure lives. Pure motives. Pure hearts. Do you think the world will really have any use for Christians until we can be committed to living according to the standards of Jesus Christ?

We all experience criticism; perhaps some of it is justified, and I would imagine some is not. Regardless, the way we will silence it is by being committed to living the way Paul challenged his spiritual son, Timothy, to live.

MORE, PLEASE!

(Additional reading)

Safe People by Dr. Henry Cloud and Dr. John Townsend

Undaunted by Christine Caine

Scars and Stilettos by Harmony Dust

Battlefield of the Mind by Joyce Meyer

How People Grow by Dr. Henry Cloud and Dr. John Townsend

10

It's All About Jesus

HOW TO GROW IN YOUR RELATIONSHIP WITH GOD

You will find as you look back upon your life that the moments you have really lived are the moments when you have done things in the spirit of love.

HENRY DRUMMOND

THE MOST IMPORTANT DECISION YOU'LL EVER MAKE

People make hundreds, if not thousands, of choices every single day. Yikes! That's a lot of decisions! What to wear, what to eat for lunch, which classes to take, whether to say yes or no to that cute guy asking you out on a date, which freeway to take for a shorter commute on the way home . . . As young women, we also have a significant number of *really important* decisions to make. Where to go to school, what career to pursue, to whom to say "I do," when to start the small business, when to start the family, whether or not to forgive, how to invest our finances . . .

Even though these are all very important decisions, there is one decision that is even more significant. It is the decision that will determine the course of your life from here into eternity.

It is the most important decision you'll ever make.

We've all contemplated making this decision before. We've asked ourselves, *Why am I here? What's the point of everything? Do I serve a greater purpose? Is there a real God? If there is, what is He really like? How does He explain the state of the world today?* And perhaps the most personal question of all: *How does God feel about me?*

Jesus offers this answer to our questions: "For God loved the world so much that he gave his one and only Son, so that everyone who believes in him will not perish but have eternal life" (John 3:16, NLT). *THE MESSAGE* puts Jesus' words this way:

> This is how much God loved the world: He gave his Son, his one and only Son. And this is why: so that no one need be destroyed; by believing in him, anyone can have a whole and lasting life. God didn't go to all the

> trouble of sending his Son merely to point an accusing finger, telling the world how bad it was. He came to help, to put the world right again (vv. 16-17).

The great news is that Jesus gives us an answer to our questions: God, our heavenly Father, loves us . . . and He has great plans and purposes for us!

In fact, God loves you so much that He gave His one and only Son, Jesus Christ, for you! The Bible says Jesus, fully God and fully man, came to earth from heaven and lived a blameless life. He willingly allowed Himself to be beaten and crucified on the cross so that you and I might have authentic, intimate relationship with God. On the cross, He became the sacrifice for our sins, our mistakes and our failures. Not only did He die for us, but three days later Jesus also rose from the dead! He conquered sin AND death to offer us a new start with God!

Jesus did all this because God passionately loves you and wants you to experience life with Him—eternal life. He wants nothing more than to have a real relationship with you! He created you with eternity in mind! He wants to be with you and care for you—in this life and in heaven—but the only way to experience life with God is through faith in Jesus.

Perhaps, you have never made the decision to open your heart and life to Jesus—to turn from your own way of doing life and instead choose to accept Him as your Lord and Savior, and begin following Him. Perhaps, at one time you made this decision, but honestly, now you feel very far from God.

Today—this moment—is your opportunity to make the decision to follow Jesus! It is the best decision you will ever make, and you can make it right now!

Simply believe in your heart that Jesus is your Lord and Savior, and pray this prayer inviting Him into your heart:

God the Father, thank You so much for sending your Son, Jesus, to pay the price for my sins—a price I could never pay. Thank You for loving me so much that Jesus died on the cross and rose from the dead for me. I accept Your love. I accept Your forgiveness. From this moment on, I am a new person—a follower of Jesus Christ. I accept Jesus as Lord and Savior of my life. Let Your Spirit lead me and guide me as I follow You all the days of my life. In Jesus' name, amen.

Congratulations! All of heaven is throwing a party for you right now! You just made the most important decision of your life!

WELCOME TO THE FAMILY

You are a member of God's very own family . . . and you belong in God's household with every other Christian.

EPHESIANS 2:19, TLB

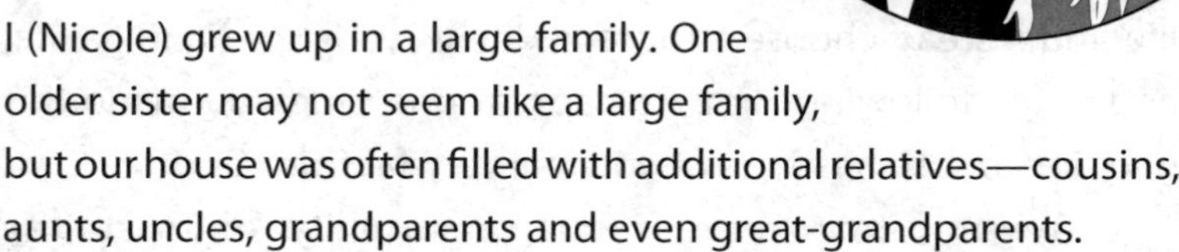

I (Nicole) grew up in a large family. One older sister may not seem like a large family, but our house was often filled with additional relatives—cousins, aunts, uncles, grandparents and even great-grandparents.

We weren't exactly what you would call a "reserved" family. "Loud" and "crazy" would be more accurate words to describe our family functions. There were always a lot of laughs, a ton of food, and an occasional brawl that somehow seemed to end with more laughter and new memories. I told you—loud and crazy! ☻

Maybe you can relate. Or maybe you had a quiet family . . . or a distant family . . . or a dysfunctional family . . . or a loving family . . . or an all-of-the-above family.

As Christ-followers, we are also included in another family—the family of God. Through faith in Jesus, we have become sons and daughters of the most high God, adopted as His very own. That makes each of us siblings in Christ. We are now a part of God's family—or as the Bible calls it, the Church.

The Church isn't a building; the Church is something far more magnificent. It's you and I united together to worship Jesus and spread the great news about His love.

We are part of something much larger than we can see or comprehend. We are among the countless many around the world who, for more than 2,000 years, have been (and are now) called the family of God!

You may not have realized it until now, but your family just grew a whole lot!

The Bible describes this family, when united together, as the showcase of God's glory to a fallen world. It is through His Church that Jesus brings love and hope to the hurting, dying and broken all around us. It is through His Church that people hear the good news of Jesus and His love for each and every one—the kind of love that cares for the orphan and the widow, and provides shelter for the homeless, freedom for the addicted, joy for the suicidal, healing for the brokenhearted, and justice for the oppressed! The loving and united Church provides the kind of Christlike love that transforms lives for all eternity!

Here's the best part . . . YOU! You are a part of this family—a unique and important part! God gave you specific talents, abilities, passions and experiences, and they are to be shared in His Church for His purposes!

No one can replace you in this family of God! You are one of a kind!

You may never have set foot in a church before . . . or maybe it's been a very long time since you have. Maybe your idea of church is a stuffy place full of critical or hypocritical people. Maybe you've even been deeply hurt by an experience at church. (We're truly sorry for that.) Maybe church is something you never really connected with or thought much about.

But you need a place where you can connect with other genuine Christ-followers, so make the bold decision to find a church you can call home! It may take some time and effort to find a local church you can be a part of, but as you pray and take the steps to find *your* church, the Holy Spirit will lead you to the right spot for His blessing!

As we noted previously, Psalm 92:12-13 tells us, "The righteous will flourish like a palm tree, they will grow like a cedar of Lebanon; planted in the house of the Lord, they will flourish in the courts of our God." And Hebrews 10:24-25 encourages us to "think of ways to motivate one another to acts of love and good works. And let us not neglect our meeting together, as some people do, but encourage one another, especially now that the day of his return is drawing near" (NLT).

The Bible promises that when we plant ourselves in a healthy local church home, our lives will flourish, and our faith will be encouraged. When we connect with the family of God and become contributing members, we discover and fulfill the great purposes God has for each of us!

So whether you've never attended church before or you are currently a part of a great local church, make sure you commit to being an active member in God's family! You were never meant to do life alone . . . you were created to be a part of the family of God!

IT'S TIME TO TALK!

Think about the people closest to you. They're the people you make time to talk with, right? You swap stories about your days over a cup of coffee. You laugh over memories shared at the dinner table. You talk for hours on the phone with your friend  from college.

You have meaningful conversations with the people you love. Your ability to communicate is one of the things that keeps your relationships strong and exciting!

The same could be said about prayer. When we consistently pray, we are building a great relationship with Jesus!

Prayer isn't as complicated as we might think it is. Prayer is simply talking and listening to your heavenly Father. You can pray when you wake up, on the way to work, before a big meeting or a hot date ☻, or before you head to bed to catch your beauty sleep. You can pray by yourself, with family, with friends, or even with someone you just met! You can pray in your room, in your car, at the office, at church, at the dinner table, or at the grocery store. You can pray for 5 minutes, you can pray for 20 minutes, or you can pray for an hour. When you pray, you can say, "Thanks!" You can praise God! You can ask for His help. You can believe for miracles. You can seek direction and guidance. And you can listen to discover God's will for your life.

When we pray, God hears us, and He responds . . . but the only way to get answered prayer is to *pray*! ☻

When we pray, not only do we invite God's blessing, but we also get to know our Savior more, which is the greatest gift of all. Through prayer, we deepen our relationships with Jesus!

Make time to pray every day, and build the relationship with Jesus you were born to have!

> The earnest (heartfelt, continued) prayer of a righteous man makes tremendous power available [dynamic in its working] (Jas. 5:16, AMP).

THE BIBLE: YOUR NAVIGATION SYSTEM

Of all the books I (Holly) have read, none has shaped my life as much as the Bible has. The interesting thing about the Bible is that while much of it contains stories about other people and other events, it is very personal. Too many people, perhaps, keep their Bibles on the shelf and never allow God to speak to them through the Scriptures.

God's Word is His voice. My time with God always involves reading His Word. As I read the Bible, it is as if God is inviting me into His very

big world and opening up the possibility that His world can become my own. It is not a question of how much I read, but rather of how I let His Word shape my day. Some days I read several chapters, while other days I focus in on just a few verses.

God will probably not speak to you in an audible voice or use skywriting or a message in a bottle to give you direction. He will speak to you through His Word.

His Word is your map for living. It is your GPS. It is your navigation system. When you are taking a road trip and plan on arriving at a specific destination, you probably don't just point your car in any direction and go. No, I imagine you have a plan. Well, God's Word is your plan for life. Without it, you will never arrive where you want to go. It is very easy to get lost on the highway of life . . . but not if you are using His Word as your guide.

HOW TO GET THE MOST OUT OF YOUR BIBLE READING

1. Pick up a **Bible Devotional** to start each day with. Devotionals focus on a short passage of Scripture and provide creative ways for you to reflect on what that passage means. After reading only a couple of pages, you will have begun your day with the Word of God as your guide.

2. Find a Bible verse to help you with a situation you are facing right now. (Maybe you can use one included in this book.) Write the verse on an **index card** and carry it with you in your purse or stick it on your bathroom mirror. Make sure to read it a few times a day. Think about what this verse means for your life, and how it changes the way you think about God, yourself, others, and even your circumstances.

3. Pick a verse that stood out to you in your Bible reading and **memorize** it. It will strengthen your faith and give you new words to pray and focus on!

4. Have you ever wondered what God thinks about something??? Why do some people seem to be happier in life than others? What does God really think about money? How does God want me to treat that annoying co-worker? ☻ Does Jesus really forgive me for *everything*? Try a **topic study** and get the answers you are looking for (and discover new questions to be asking along the way!). Simply use a basic concordance (many Bibles have one located in the back) or try out the Topical Index or Keyword Search functions on www.biblegateway.com. Look up or type in a basic topic to get started. You can narrow your search to a particular book or portion of the Bible (such as the New Testament), or you can search the entire Bible. I recommend using the *New International Version* or

New Living Translation for a topic search. If you're not sure where to start, you could give one of these topics a try: patience, joy, obedience, friendship, courage, discipline, forgiveness, giving, healing, integrity, kindness or thanksgiving. Some studies may take an hour or so. Others you may continue exploring for a week, or even a month, in your daily time of reading the Bible.

5. Read a **psalm** or a **proverb** a day as part of your daily Bible reading. The psalms are beautifully written prayers and songs of praise and worship to God that help us develop a passionate, loyal love for Jesus. The proverbs are a collection of wise sayings that give us clear and practical direction about how to live life God's way.

6. Read through a **Gospel** in a month by reading a chapter a day. The Gospels—Matthew, Mark, Luke and John—are written accounts of the life of Jesus found in the New Testament. They include His teachings, His miracles, His interactions with His disciples and others, His death and His resurrection. As we learn more about Jesus, we ultimately discover more of the heart of our heavenly Father toward us!

7. Check out **study companions** to accompany you in your Bible reading. There are resources that assist you

in different types of Bible study; commentaries that offer additional insight to your Bible reading; and books that further explore themes, characters and historical context in the Bible.

8. Have you ever wanted to read the whole Bible cover to cover??? Find a **Bible Reading Plan** online, and decide to read the New Testament or the entire Bible in a year. By reading only a few chapters a day, you'll be able to complete the Bible in just a year's time!

9. Purchase a **journal**, and take notes while reading the Bible. Write down verses that stand out to you. Jot down thoughts about God, yourself and others that are sparked by what you read. List action steps you are going to take based on what you found in the Bible. You can even write out prayers to God that a particular part of the Bible inspired you to pray. Every month or so, take 30 minutes to read what you've written in your journal and reflect on all the great things the Holy Spirit is showing you and doing in your life!

10. Read a chapter of the Bible in three or four **different translations**. Compare verses that stand out to you. This is a great way to gain a fuller understanding of what you are reading. You can find various translations of the Bible available for free at www.biblegateway.com.

Bible Translation Formula:
New International Version (standard)
+ THE MESSAGE (modern paraphrase)
+ Amplified (lots of words)
+ New American Standard Bible (standard) =
AWESOME TIME SPENT IN THE BIBLE

11. **Find a consistent time and place** to read your Bible every day as part of your time spent with God. Give yourself enough time to really connect with Jesus. Transform your space into a distraction-free zone (no TV, no phone calls, no interruptions). This may mean waking up early or finding a secluded spot during your lunch break or locking yourself in your bedroom with a "DO NOT DISTURB" sign for your roommates to read! ☻

12. **Pray!** Pray before, during and after reading your Bible! Pray before, thanking God for sharing His thoughts with you through the Bible. Pray during, asking the Holy Spirit to give you understanding of the verse or passage you are reading. Pray after you are done reading, asking God to make it personal for you! Ask the Holy Spirit to show you how you can realign your thoughts to the thoughts of His that you have just discovered in the Bible . . . and how you can practically apply what you have just read to your situation or circumstances!

TWELVE PRETTY AWESOME THINGS JESUS DID (AND WHAT THEY TELL US ABOUT GOD)

1. **Jesus declared He was the Son of God and the only way to eternal life** (see John 14:6-7). God sent His Son, Jesus, to provide salvation for each of us. Jesus was more than a good man or a great prophet; He was—and is—the Son of God. It is only through faith in Jesus that we are able to have a genuine relationship with God and receive eternal salvation.

2. **Jesus preached a different way of life** (see Matt. 5-7). God wants to teach us how to live: how to love one another, how to forgive, how to manage our finances, how to worship God, and how to discover our purposes. His way for your life is the best way for your life! By following the direction for your life that He gives in the Bible, you will begin to live out the great life God has planned for you!

3. **Jesus ate with tax collectors and sinners** (see Mark 2:15-16). God doesn't expect us to be perfect before we can be in relationship with Him. He forgives us and accepts us as His children no matter what we have done! God desires an authentic relationship—one in which we are accepted and loved as we are!

4. **Jesus turned water into wine** (see John 2:1-11). God loves to have a good time! He wants us to live with joy and celebration regardless of our situations or circumstances.

5. **Jesus healed the sick** (see Matt. 12:15). God does not want anyone to be physically or emotionally sick. He doesn't punish us with sickness and His desire is to heal us!

6. **Jesus cast out demons** (see Matt. 8:16). God is all-powerful—more powerful than the enemy of our souls—and He has given us freedom and healing from hurts, bad habits and addictions.

7. **Jesus multiplied a couple of tuna fish sandwiches to feed thousands** (see Matt. 14:13-21). God provides for us, both spiritually and physically. When we trust Him with our resources and finances, He miraculously provides for us and always meets our needs!

8. **Jesus calmed storms and even walked on water!** (see Matt. 8:23-27 and Matt. 14:25-27). God is not a distant God who leaves us

to figure things out on our own. When the storms of life come our way, we can pray to God! When we do that, we can rely on His power and strength to give us peace, wisdom and provision for whatever storm we are facing!

9. **Jesus defended the cause of the poor and marginalized** (see Matt. 5:3 and John 8:7). God is a God of justice, and He cares for the hurting and marginalized. He is moved with compassion for the poor, the sick, the ignored and the abandoned. He desires that you and I each do our part to care for and fight for those who are experiencing injustice in our communities and in our world.

10. **Jesus died on the cross for our sins** (see John 3:16 and Mark 8:31). God has offered each of us salvation through Jesus. On the cross, He paid the price for your sins, mistakes and failures, and it is through faith in Him that you are saved. You can't earn God's love; He gives it freely!

11. **Jesus rose from the dead!** (see Luke 24:6). God is more powerful than death itself! As believers in Jesus, we no longer have to fear death—because we are confident that we are heaven-bound!

12. **Jesus gave us His Spirit to continue His work!** (see Matt. 28:18-20). God sends His very Spirit to reside

in our hearts when we believe in Jesus. His Spirit gives us the power to experience His great love for us and to live out the great purposes He has for us as His children.

GOD'S WORD FOR YOU . . .

Healing. "Jesus turned and saw her. 'Take heart, daughter,' he said, 'your faith has healed you.' And the woman was healed from that moment" (Matt. 9:22).

Peace. "Don't fret or worry. Instead of worrying, pray. Let petitions and praises shape your worries into prayers, letting God know your concerns. Before you know it, a sense of God's wholeness, everything coming together for good, will come and settle you down. It's wonderful what happens when Christ displaces worry at the center of your life" (Phil. 4:6-7, THE MESSAGE).

Courage. "There is no fear in love; but perfect love casts out fear, because fear involves torment" (1 John 4:18, NKJV).

Strength. "But those who hope in the Lord will renew their strength. They will soar on wings like eagles; they will run and not grow weary, they will walk and not be faint" (Isa. 40:31).

Hope. "'For I know the plans I have for you,' says the Lord. 'They are plans for good and not for disaster, to give you a future and a hope'" (Jer. 29:11, NLT).

Joy. "I'm singing joyful praise to God. I'm turning cartwheels of joy to my Savior God. Counting on God's Rule to prevail, I take heart and gain strength. I run like a deer. I feel like I'm king of the mountain!" (Hab. 3:18-19, THE MESSAGE).

Forgiveness. "If we confess our sins, he is faithful and just and will forgive us our sins and purify us from all unrighteousness" (1 John 1:9).

Love. "And I am convinced that nothing can ever separate us from God's love. Neither death nor life, neither angels nor demons, neither our fears for today nor our worries about tomorrow—not even the powers of hell can separate us from God's love. No power in the sky above or in the earth below—indeed, nothing in all creation will ever be able to separate us from the love of God that is revealed in Christ Jesus our Lord" (Rom. 8:38-39, NLT).

OOPS! MY BAD! NOW WHAT???

You blew it. Big-time. . . . Or maybe not big-time, but enough to feel bad about it. You did something you shouldn't have. You lied to someone who trusts you. You talked behind your boss's back. You gossiped. You went too far with your boyfriend on your last date. You gave in to an addiction you thought you had overcome.

Or maybe it's something you didn't do. You didn't tell the truth when you had the chance. You didn't defend the person you witnessed being teased. You haven't extended forgiveness to the one who wronged you. You didn't leave that party or club when you should have.

Well, here are two pieces of good news: God doesn't love you any less, and you are not alone.

That's right. God loves you. Period. You can't add to His love, and you can't diminish it. Nothing you do or don't do changes the way God feels for you. John 3:16 tells us that "God so loved the world that He gave His only begotten Son, that whoever believes in Him should not perish but have everlasting life!" (NKJV). Talk about GOOD NEWS! God proved just how much He loves you, and to what lengths He would go to be with you. He was willing to sacrifice His own Son, Jesus, on the cross for you! It's through faith in Jesus that we each get in on this life of love that God has for us!

Our failures and our mistakes don't change that. They don't change the way God feels and thinks about you or me! Nothing ever will!

Be assured, you are not alone. There are no perfect Christians roaming the planet. They certainly aren't sitting next to you at church this Sunday, even if you think they are. We all make mistakes. Romans 3:23 tells us, "For everyone has *sinned*; we all *fall short* of God's glorious standard" (NLT, emphasis added). We all need God's grace and forgiveness . . . and He is faithful to give it!

So when we make mistakes, what do we do? Well, we certainly don't sweep them under the rug. We don't shrug our shoulders and just forget about it. Neither do we have to feel overwhelmingly guilty and undeserving of God's love.

When we make a mistake (the Bible calls this "sin"), here are a few easy steps we can take to move past our big "oops-moment." I call them "The 4 Rs of Moving On."

1. **Recognize** that the Holy Spirit, out of love, is convicting your heart about something you have done or thought (or something you have chosen NOT to do or think) that doesn't honor God.

2. **Rely** on forgiveness. Psalm 86:5 promises us, "O Lord, you are so good, so ready to forgive, so full of unfailing love for all who ask for your help" (NLT). Ask God genuinely for forgiveness, and trust that He is quick to forgive you!

3. **Repent.** To "repent" simply means to turn from an old way and embrace a new way. Turning from an old way of doing something may mean changing habits and influences. (The Bible calls this "avoiding temptation.") It also means that you are willing to share your mistake with a mature follower of Christ. (The Bible calls this "confessing your sins one to another.") By telling this person about your "oops-moment," you invite her encouragement, support and accountability to grow and move past a mistake that is now in your past.

4. **Realign** your thinking and attitude to God's will for your life. (The Bible calls this "renewing the mind.") Discover in the Bible what God says about you and about the particular area in which you are growing. Choose to believe what God says about you, rather than base your understanding on your past or even your present circumstances!

FAN VS. FOLLOWER

Have you ever attended a large sporting event? If you're a sports fanatic or married to one—or even if you ever attended a high school football game—then you know that being a fan can be a lot of fun! You get to wear team colors and jerseys; shout and wave foam fingers; give out a lot of high fives; participate in "the wave"; consume more than the normally recommended amount of hot dogs, soft pretzels and nachos; and create hilarious and unpredictable memories with friends and family. You get to pick and choose your favorite players, critique athletic performances, and argue with a referee's call. Fun, right?!

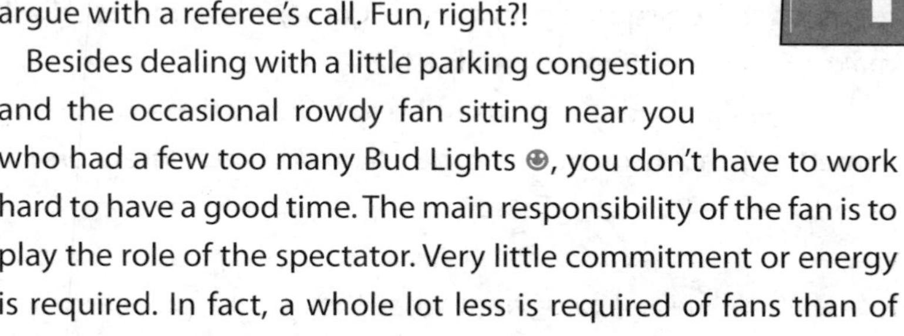

Besides dealing with a little parking congestion and the occasional rowdy fan sitting near you who had a few too many Bud Lights ☻, you don't have to work hard to have a good time. The main responsibility of the fan is to play the role of the spectator. Very little commitment or energy is required. In fact, a whole lot less is required of fans than of actual players. Think about it:

Fans	Players
Fans sit on the sidelines.	Players get in on the action of the field.
Fans critique.	Players contribute.
Fans' enthusiasm is easily swayed.	Players' passion is immovable.
Fans show up to games when it's convenient.	Players show up prepared for every game.
Fans aren't on a team roster.	Players work as a team under the direction of the coach.
Fans don't break a sweat.	Players train to win.
Fans buy T-shirts.	Players bring home championship trophies.

You get the idea.

While being a fan can be fun when it comes to sporting events and concerts, it's not exactly the kind of life Jesus had in mind for us when He issued the invitation: "Come, follow me, and I will make you fishers of men" (Mark 1:17).

Jesus never intended for us to be *fans*; instead, He calls us to something much greater—to be His *followers (players on His team)*... Luke 9:23-25 tells us:

> Then he [Jesus] told them what they could expect for themselves: "Anyone who intends to come with me

> has to let me lead. You're not in the driver's seat—I am. Don't run from suffering; embrace it. Follow me and I'll show you how. Self-help is no help at all. Self-sacrifice is the way, my way, to finding yourself, your true self. What good would it do to get everything you want and lose you, the real you?" (THE MESSAGE).

What Jesus is calling us to is life not as a fan but as a true follower. We were never meant to be spectators of faith, but active players winning for God's kingdom.

Refuse to spend your life on the sidelines! Get on the field and live out the God-adventure set in place for you before the beginning of time! Make Jesus the number one priority of your life! Pursue Him at all costs! Each and every day, make the powerful choice to be a true follower of Jesus! Only then will you discover the life you've always wanted to live!

THIS LITTLE LIGHT OF MINE . . .

"This little light of mine, I'm gonna let it shine." (Sing it with me if you know it! ☻ "This little light of mine, I'm gonna let it shine. This little light of mine, I'm gonna let it shine, let it shine, let it shine, let it shine!"[1]

If you ever went to Sunday School as a kid, chances are you've heard this gospel song. It's a song sprinkled with nostalgia. It's the kind of song you could watch a freckled two-year-old with pigtails sing on YouTube. It's guaranteed to stir up warm and fuzzy feelings in even the most disgruntled and grumpy individuals.

But the message in this song is far more significant than simply offering a trip down memory lane or a sense of innocence in the world today.

Instead, this song speaks to a great mandate that you and I have been given by Jesus Himself! It's a call to a life of meaning and mission . . .

Listen to Jesus' words from Matthew 5:14-16:

> You're here to be light, bringing out the God-colors in the world. God is not a secret to be kept. We're going public with this, as public as a city on a hill. If I make you light-bearers, you don't think I'm going to hide you under a bucket, do you? I'm putting you on a light stand. Now that I've put you there on a hilltop, on a light stand—shine! Keep open house; be generous with your lives. By opening up to others, you'll prompt people to open up with God, this generous Father in heaven (THE MESSAGE).

To quote another translation, Jesus calls us "the light of the world" (v. 14, NIV)! We are meant to shine brightly—so brightly, in fact, that the darkest places are exposed to God-colors! Our light is meant to reflect the Light of the world, our Savior Jesus!

We shine brightest when we love and show value to others. When we pick up a coffee for a coworker, when we help a friend move into a new apartment, when we buy groceries for a neighbor who is experiencing financial strain, when we forgive the ex who betrayed us, when we speak highly rather than poorly of someone when she or he is not around—well, it's in these simple, daily acts that we truly SHINE!

We become a light that causes the people in our world to pause and take notice; whether or not they know God, they are drawn to the illumination of our lives. It is then that we get the opportunity to share with others what Jesus has done in our lives. We simply tell our stories—the stories God is authoring in our lives . . . what He has saved us from, how our lives have changed since embarking on a relationship with Jesus, and how we continue to experience His love and grace.

When we shine, things change—or more accurately, people change. People are introduced to the heart-transforming love of Jesus! Ultimately, when we shine, we aren't shining our own light, but the light that comes from Jesus Himself living in our hearts! We are merely reflectors of God's miraculous and magnificent light! It's through the Holy Spirit at work in us that we have the strength and courage to shine!

Don't hide. Refuse to live timid. You were born to shine! Shine! Shine in your family! Shine in your school! Shine in your workplace! Shine in your community! Shine in this world! It's waiting to be lit with God-colors by YOU!

MORE, PLEASE!

(Additional reading)

He Chose the Nails by Max Lucado

GodChicks Awakened by Holly Wagner

Rick Warren's Bible Study Methods by Rick Warren

The Jesus I Never Knew by Philip Yancey

Lord, Teach Me to Study the Bible in 28 Days by Kay Arthur

The Life You've Always Wanted by John Ortberg

Too Busy Not to Pray by Bill Hybels

ENDNOTES

CHAPTER 1: WHY AM I HERE? HOW TO DISCOVER YOUR GOD-GIVEN PURPOSE

1. Thom S. Rainer, *The Unchurched Next Door* (Grand Rapids, MI: Zondervan, 2003), p. 24.
2. "11 Facts About Dropping Out," www.dosomething.org/tipsandtools/11-facts-about-dropping-out (accessed February 2012).
3. "A Generation At Risk," www.rainbows.org/statistics.html (accessed February 2012).
4. "The Need" www.generositywater.org/the-need (accessed March 2012).

CHAPTER 2: ONE OF A KIND: HOW TO CELEBRATE YOUR UNIQUE STYLE

1. "Hair Color," http://www.my-virtual-makeover.com/hair-color.html (accessed April 2012).
2. Viktoria Love, "A Fashionistas Guide—Emergency Wardrobe Kit," April 30, 2011, http://viktorialove.com/2011/04/30/a-fashionistas-guide-emergency-wardrobe-kit/ (accessed April 2012).

CHAPTER 3: HEALTHY LIVING: HOW TO LIVE LONG AND LOOK GOOD

1. Susan Goodwin, "Why is Omega 3 Good For You?" http://ezinearticles.com/?Why-is-Omega-3-Good-For-You?&id=4505704 (accessed December 2011).
2. "6 Health Benefits of Black Beans," May 29, 2011, http://www.healthdiaries.com/eatthis/6-health-benefits-of-black-beans.html (accessed December 2011).
3. "All the Health Risks of Processed Foods—In Just a Few Quick, Convenient Bites," http://www.sixwise.com/newsletters/05/10/19/all-the-health-risks-of-processed-foods----in-just-a-few-quick-convenient-bites.htm (accessed December 2011).
4. Adapted from "The Six Thousand Hidden Dangers of Processed Foods (and What to Choose Instead)," October 18, 2007, http://bodyecology.com/articles/hidden_dangers_of_processed_foods.php (accessed December 2011).
5. Kathleen M. Zelman, MPH, RD, LD, "The Skinny on Fat: Good Fats vs. Bad Fats," November 1, 2007, http://www.webmd.com/diet/features/skinny-fat-good-fats-bad-fats? (accessed December 2011).
6. Ibid.
7. Shelley Levitt, "6 Secrets to Gorgeous Skin," August 18, 2011, http://www.webmd.com/healthy-beauty/features/tips-for-gorgeous-skin (accessed January 2012).
8. Mayo Clinic staff, "Exercise: 7 benefits of regular physical activity," http://www.mayoclinic.com/health/exercise/HQ01676/ (accessed December 2011).
9. Eric R. Braverman, M.D., with Dale Kiefer, B.S., "Combating Age-Related Brain Deterioration," *Life Extension Magazine*, http://www.lef.org/magazine/mag2011/oct2011_Combating-Age-Related-Brain-Deterioration_02.htm (accessed December 2011).
10. Mayo Clinic staff, "Stress relievers: Top 10 picks to tame stress," http://www.mayoclinic.com/health/stress-relievers/MY01373/ (accessed December 2011).
11. Joseph E. Pizzorno, Jr., and Michael T. Murray, *Textbook of Natural Medicine*, 3rd ed. (St. Louis: Churchill Livingstone, 2006), vol. 1, pp. 701–708.
12. "Brain Basics: Understanding Sleep," National Institute of Neurological Disorders and Stroke, http://www.ninds.nih.gov/disorders/brain_basics/understanding_sleep.htm (accessed January 2012).

13. "Aging Alters Sleep and Hormone Levels Sooner Than Expected," University of Chicago report, August 15, 2000, http://www.uchospitals.edu/news/2000/20000815-soma.html (accessed April 2012).

14. Jordan Rubin, *The Great Physician's Rx for Health and Wellness* (Nashville, TN: Thomas Nelson, 2006), p. 150.

15. "Myths, Truths and Looking Good," *20/20*, February 18, 2005, http://abcnews.go.com/Health/2020/story?id=512095 (accessed April 2012).

16. "Sleep position gives personality clue," *BBC News*, September 16, 2003, http://news.bbc.co.uk/2/hi/health/3112170.stm (accessed January 2012).

17. Melinda Smith, M.A.; Lawrence Robinson; Joanna Saisan, M.S.W.; and Robert Segal, M.A., "How to Sleep Better," December 2011, http://www.helpguide.org/life/sleep_tips.htm (accessed February 2012).

18. *The Great Physician's Rx for Health and Wellness*, p. 45.

19. Don Colbert, M.D., *The Seven Pillars of Health*, (Lake Mary, FL: Siloam, 2007), p. 12.

20. F. Batmanghelidj, M.D., *You're Not Sick, You're Thirsty!* (New York: Warner Books, 2003), pp. 225-226.

21. *The Great Physician's Rx for Health and Wellness*, p. 47.

22. Ibid., p. 154.

23. Ibid., pp. 154-155.

CHAPTER 4: WHAT'S IN YOUR WALLET? HOW TO MANAGE FINANCES

1. Dave Ramsey, *Dave Ramsey's Financial Peace University* (Brentwood, TN: The Lampo Group, 2008), p. 71.

2. Ibid., p. 72.

CHAPTER 5: DOING LIFE TOGETHER: HOW TO NAVIGATE FRIENDSHIPS

1. Eugene H. Peterson, *Five Smooth Stones for Pastoral Work* (Grand Rapids, MI: Wm. B. Eerdmans Publishing Co., 1980), p. 192.

2. Leslie Guerrero Collins, L.M.T., "Relax with Laughter," http://absolutelyrelaxedaustin.health.officelive.com/RelaxwithLaughter.aspx (accessed February 2012).

CHAPTER 7: TYING THE KNOT: BUILDING A MARRIAGE THAT LASTS

1. Margaret K. Scarf, "Remarriage Is More Fragile Than First Marriage," in *The Bonus Years of Adulthood, Psychology Today*, January 12, 2009, http://www.psychologytoday.com/blog/the-bonus-years-adulthood/200901/remarriage-is-more-fragile-first-marriage (accessed April 2012).

2. Dr. Robin L. Smith, *Lies at the Altar* (New York: Hyperion, 2006).

CHAPTER 8: MODERN FAMILY: HOW TO MAINTAIN A HEALTHY HOUSEHOLD

1. Deanne C. Haisch, M.A., LMHP, "Giving Good Instructions to Children," parenting.org from Boys Town, http://www.parenting.org/article/giving-good-instructions-children (accessed February 2012).

CHAPTER 10: IT'S ALL ABOUT JESUS: HOW TO GROW IN YOUR RELATIONSHIP WITH GOD

1. Harry Dixon Loes, "This Little Light of Mine," www.hymns.me.uk/this-little-light-of-mine-favorite-hymn.htm (accessed February 2012).

ALSO BY
HOLLY WAGNER

Daily Steps for GodChicks
ISBN 978.08307.42059

GodChicks Awakened
ISBN 978.08307.57503

GodChicks and the Men They Love
with Philip Wagner
ISBN 978.08307.52386

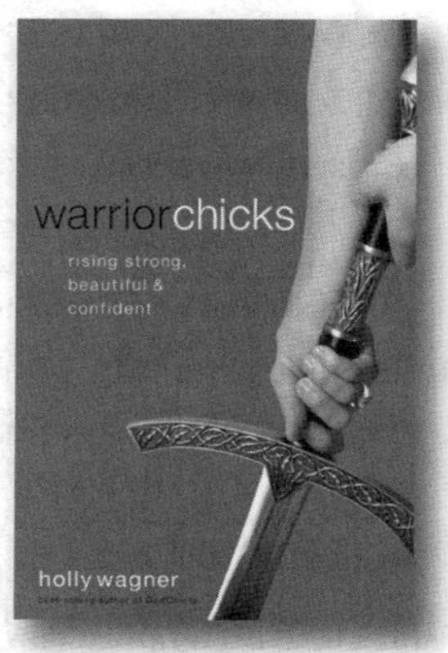

Warrior Chicks
ISBN 978.08307.44800